INTERMEDIATE CEFR B1-B2

English at the Speed of TECH

EFFECTIVE COMMUNICATION FOR GLOBAL TEAMS

KRIS ESPLIN

Dedicated to Eiko Esplin, whose love, patience, and commitment to lifelong learning have inspired this series.

Acknowledgments:

I am very grateful to the many people who helped make this textbook possible. Your ideas, feedback, and support were invaluable.

First, I would like to thank Everett Ofori for his encouragement and support when I was first shaping the ideas behind this book. Your experience, advice, and enthusiasm helped give the project early direction.

My sincere thanks go to Diana Camargo, Eric Altman, John Cunningham, Marish Mackowiak, and Randall Grace for reviewing early drafts and sharing thoughtful suggestions, encouragement, and moral support. Your positive feedback kept me motivated throughout.

A special thank you to Jeremy Hyatt and Everett, who went above and beyond by carefully checking the vocabulary activities to ensure they were accurate, clear, and meaningful. Your attention to detail raised the overall quality of the text.

I would also like to thank David Baird, Diana, Eric, John, and Marish for their help proofreading the final drafts. Your care and dedication were invaluable during the final stages.

Finally, to everyone mentioned here—and to those whose contributions may not be listed but were just as important—thank you. This textbook reflects the support, effort, and generosity of many people, and I am deeply grateful to all of you for being part of this project.

ENGLISH AT THE SPEED OF TECH
Effective Communication for Global Teams

About the Book

Welcome to English at the Speed of TECH, a course designed for adult EFL business English learners working on global teams in the tech industry. This book aims to elevate your language ability, ensuring you can communicate more effectively in the fast-paced, dynamic world of Big Tech.

Key Features

1. Practical Business Language and Skills: Unlocks essential language and skills tailored to the tech sector. Whether you need to exchange information, actively participate in discussions, or drive business outcomes, our comprehensive approach to more effective communication has you covered.

2. Spaced Repetition for more Effective Learning: As a working professional, your time is a valued asset. That's why this book incorporates spaced repetition, a proven learning technique, to help you maximize your language proficiency. Key vocabulary and grammar concepts are strategically reintroduced throughout the book, reinforcing long-term memory and retention.

3. Versatile Learning Paths: Adapt to your learning style, either as a self-directed journey using the text as a personalized workbook, or opt for an interactive experience by partnering with a teacher, colleague, or peer. The included expansion activities are ideal for refining your spoken communication abilities by focusing on realistic simulations and engaging role-plays. **Free 'Teacher Notes' are also available for additional examples and guided practice** (see simulation 'Pro-Tips' for contact information).

Elevate Your Game: Experience a journey where language proficiency meets practicality, empowering you to excel in Big Tech's business communication landscape. With this book as your guide, you'll gain the confidence and skills needed to navigate the complexities of the tech industry and communicate more effectively in English.

About the Author

Kris Esplin, the author of English at the Speed of TECH, has over 25 years experience in EFL corporate training and holds an MA in TESOL from Teachers College, Columbia University. Kris has taught and  developed content across various levels and business sectors in Japan for almost 30 years, specializing in learner-centered business English and ESP programs. Kris also holds certifications in Mac OS Server Administration and CISA (ISACA), and has experience as an IT Manager and Auditor for ISMS and ISO27001 compliance. With a strong educational background and extensive experience in content development and IT management, Kris is well-equipped to create content tailored to the tech industry. Currently based in Tokyo, Kris is coaching students for a leading EduTech company.

ENGLISH AT THE SPEED OF TECH

Table of Contents

ENGLISH AT THE SPEED OF TECH

UNIT | 01 The Language of Innovation

LEARNING OBJECTIVES

In Unit 1: The Language of Innovation, you'll dive into key tech terms and phrases essential for discussions about innovation in the tech industry. You'll learn to more confidently use these terms in everyday business contexts, discuss tech trends and processes with ease, and understand the basics of tech conversations. This unit sets the foundation for effective communication in Big Tech, enhancing your ability to engage with global teams and innovate within your field.

Unit 1 Task 1

WARM-UP

Take a minute to think about the questions below. Try to predict what this unit is going to discuss and how it might benefit your work or company. Note down your predictions; we will use these ideas as a starting point for our deep dive into the power of technology in business innovation:

- How might embracing innovation support your current role?
- How could the integration of AI in your daily tasks impact your workflow?

DID YOU KNOW...

"... the iPhone, now a tech industry titan, initially faced significant challenges that could have impacted its success? These included an exclusive partnership with AT&T, the lack of an App Store at launch, and a very high price point at the time. Adding to the drama, Steve Jobs reportedly kept a prototype in his back pocket to demonstrate its durability, but it was prone to scratches, forcing a last-minute move to a glass screen. Despite these obstacles, the iPhone's innovative touch interface and Apple's marketing strategy made it the most successful product in tech history."

ENGLISH AT THE SPEED OF TECH

UNIT 01 The Language of Innovation

KEY VOCABULARY IN CONTEXT

disruptive (adj), prototype (n), scalable (adj), benchmark (n), innovate (v), patent (n), agile (adj), iterate (v), analytics (n), streamline (v)

Read the email from Teri Lee to her development team to see the words used in context.

Subject: Recent Prototype News

To: Development Team
From: Teri Lee, Director of Innovation
Date: November 11, 202x

Dear Team,

Our commitment to *innovate* has produced a *prototype* that's set to be *disruptive* in the fintech sector. Its *scalable* architecture aligns well with our growth strategy and puts us ahead of the competition.

Current *analytics* show that performance is above key industry *benchmarks*. This success is largely due to our *agile* development process that lets us *iterate* features based on user feedback.

We're also in the process of securing a *patent* for our unique encryption algorithm. Along with this, efforts to *streamline* the deployment pipeline are underway, promising even faster delivery times.

Your continued support is much appreciated as we refine our innovation process.

Best,

Teri Lee

PRO-TIP: Which words have you seen or heard somewhere before, but aren't completely sure about what they mean or how to use them? Focusing on such words is a proven learning strategy that is supported by language experts. It's about building on what you're already familiar with first. This approach is not only smart, but is also efficient – revisiting semi-familiar words regularly helps solidify them in your memory, thereby increasing your vocabulary range in a practical, manageable way.

ENGLISH AT THE SPEED OF TECH

UNIT | 01 The Language of Innovation

Unit 1 Task 3 ## KEY VOCABULARY IN CONTEXT - PRACTICE

Complete the sentences below by filling in each blank with the best word from the choices provided. The first one is done for you.

Tip: Consider the context of the sentence so the words you choose make sense.
Look for grammar clues that can help you decide which word to use. Use the process of elimination, ruling out words until you find the best match.

1. The company uses an . . . . approach for quick adaptation to market shifts.

| A. streamline | **B. agile** | C. iterate |

2. Our new smartwatch . . . . uses advanced sensors for increased functionality.

| A. disruptive | B. prototype | C. scalable |

3. To stay competitive, we must continually . . . . and improve our products.

| A. agile | B. analytics | C. innovate |

4. Cloud services provide . . . . solutions for most business storage needs.

| A. scalable | B. patent | C. streamline |

5. We set a clear . . . . for energy efficiency that all devices must meet.

| A. agile | B. iterate | C. benchmark |

6. The marketing team used advanced . . . . to reveal the campaign's success.

| A. analytics | B. patent | C. streamline |

7. The legal department is filing a . . . . for our new battery design.

| A. patent | B. disruptive | C. innovate |

8. In the tech industry, ... innovations rapidly reshape consumer behavior.

| A. streamline | B. disruptive | C. analytics |

9. The engineering team plans to . . . . on the software for better performance.

| A. iterate | B. scalable | C. disruptive |

10. The new workflow should . . . . our coding processes for improved efficiency.

| A. innovative | B. analytics | C. streamline |

Answer key p.17

8

ENGLISH AT THE SPEED OF TECH

UNIT 01 The Language of Innovation

BUSINESS DIALOGUE

Read the dialogue and answer the comprehension questions that follow below.

Alan: So, we've just completed the initial prototype that's looking to be quite disruptive in the smart-home sector.

Keiko: That's exciting, Alan. To prepare for initial production and testing, we need to ensure the design is scalable.

Alan: Absolutely, scalability is key. We're also planning to set benchmarks for cost-effectiveness and ease of use.

Vikram: I've also asked Legal to start the patent process to protect this innovative IP. It's a necessary step for such a pioneering project.

Keiko: Thanks, Vikram! Alan, let's keep our processes as agile as possible. We need to adapt quickly to user feedback.

Alan: Of course! Analytics already show a positive trend in user interest, which is very promising.

Vikram: That's great, Alan! Integrating user feedback and analytics will help us streamline processes, which is vital for future iterations.

Alan: I agree. I'll organize a meeting with the dev team to review the analytics and plan out how we can iterate more effectively.

Keiko: Thanks, Alan. I'll work to ensure our production team can scale up without compromising on quality. It's going to need a team effort to get this done.

Vikram: Right! And I'll work to ensure the patent process moves forward on schedule. Shall we meet again next week to discuss progress?

Alan: Sounds good. I'll send out a summary email and next steps in an email this afternoon and will check schedules for a call early next week.

Comprehension questions

Q1   What industry is Alan's team's prototype expected to impact?

Q2   According to Keiko, why is it important for the design to be scalable?

Q3   What steps does Vikram take to protect their innovations?

Q4   What will Alan do after the meeting today?

Answer key p.18

ENGLISH AT THE SPEED OF TECH

PHRASE BANK

The phrases below are designed to help you discuss innovation and development more effectively in a professional setting. They should assist you in clearly presenting proposals, engaging with current market trends, optimizing processes, and more. Use these phrases to more confidently express your thoughts and contribute to discussions on technology and innovation at work.

Making Proposals
Aiming for a 99.9% uptime requires us to ...
To achieve an 90% score, we could ...
Addressing scalability might involve ...
In order to streamline, we should ...

Emphasizing Process Efficiency
To maintain our competitive edge, we can ...
If we want to stay agile, we must ...
For a more iterative process, we should ...
Streamlining this function could involve ...

Integrating User Feedback
Implementing beta sets now will require ...
To integrate user feedback, we should ...
Adapting to user requests might involve ...
Addressing customer needs will include ...

Justifying Decisions
Given the data results, we decided to ...
The decision to upgrade is backed by ...
Opting for this solution is justified by ...
The beta-phase decision is supported by ...

Offering Solutions
A likely solution for scalability might be ...
To address these issues, one approach is ...
We can solve the feedback bottleneck by ...
A viable solution for robust encryption is ...

Discussing Market Trends
With usage growing, we need to ...
To capitalize on the trend towards AI, let's ...
Considering eco-friendly tech, we might ...
To exploit this fintech gap, we need to ...

Discussing Technical Requirements
Handling user data will require us to ...
To ensure services are secure, we might ...
Addressing feasibility will involve ...
Upgrading encryption should include ...

Utilizing Data Analytics
Leveraging analytics to predict trends will ...
To inform iterations with analytics, means ...
Addressing user needs via data involves ...
Ranking engagement statistics requires ...

Requesting Information
Can you provide the latest figures on ...
I need more insights on our capacity to ...
Please expand on the potential impact of ...
What are the projections for growth in ...

Setting Expectations
We should expect to see results by ...
Our security upgrades will likely lead to ...
In terms of user data, we are aiming for ...
As for the patch, you should have it by ...

CULTURE TIP

"Innovation thrives on open communication in Big Tech environments. Be prepared to share your ideas and engage in collaborative brainstorming sessions, where contributions are valued regardless of rank. Embrace the culture of open dialogue, but approach it with respect and professionalism."

ENGLISH AT THE SPEED OF TECH

UNIT | 01 The Language of Innovation

GRAMMAR FOCUS: PRESENT SIMPLE

The present simple tense is used for actions that are habits or routines and for stating facts or general truths. In a business context, it's often used to describe regular procedures, company operations, and facts about products or services.

1. Our agile planning **streamlines** processes, allowing for rapid iteration of new features.

2. Our CS team **ensures** that all client feedback is addressed in a timely manner.

3. The R&D team **iterates** several versions each quarter, ensuring a stable final release.

4. The company **exceeds** industry standards for energy efficiency in all its products.

5. Open communication **helps** us to innovate and stay competitive.

> *Tip: A simple rule to remember for using the present simple tense is the '1-2-3 Rule':*
> *One for habits or routines:* Use the present simple to talk about actions that are habitual or routine. For example, "I check my email every morning."
> *Two for truths or facts:* Use it for statements that are generally true or for facts. For example, "The sun rises in the east."
> *Three for permanent situations:* Use it for situations that are permanent or for a state that does not change often. For example, "Our company sells software."
> And *a bonus tip for grammar:* For he/she/it, add an "s" to the verb. For example, "She works at a tech company."

Unit 1 Task 5

GRAMMAR PRACTICE

Change the verbs in the following sentences from their base form to the present simple tense. Remember the "1-2-3 Rule": Use the present simple for habitual actions (1), general truths (2), and permanent situations (3). For sentences with "he," "she," or "it" as the subject, don't forget to add an "s" to the verb.

1. He . . . . (innovate) new solutions as part of his R&D work.

2. The software . . . . (to streamline) the data processing workflow.

3. She . . . . (to hold) a patent for an eco-friendly battery.

4. It . . . . (to iterate) through different designs before finalizing.

5. Our company . . . . (to use) analytics to understand consumer behavior.

6. They . . . . (to work) on prototypes until they are complete.

7. The new application . . . . (to make) shopping easier for users.

8. She . . . . (to manage) her team efficiently and effectively.

9. The server . . . . (to process) thousands of transactions each second.

10. He . . . . (to attend) the annual tech conference every September.

Answer key p.18

ENGLISH AT THE SPEED OF TECH

UNIT 01 The Language of Innovation

GRAMMAR IN ACTION

Read through the sentences below and underline the verbs in the present simple tense. Consider how the verbs are used to describe regular actions, general truths, or routines. The first one is done for you.

Affirmative Statements

• The software automatically _**updates**_ whenever a new feature becomes available.

• Engineers regularly integrate the latest technologies into our product designs.

• Our website supports user interaction through intuitive navigation.

Negative Statements

• The company doesn't compromise on quality in its quest for innovation.

• Our data analysis tool doesn't overlook any anomalies in the datasets.

• The programming language doesn't require manual memory management.

Questions

• Does the new platform facilitate remote collaboration for global teams?

• Do all employees have access to the innovation lab?

• What advantages does this approach offer over traditional methods?

Frequency

• Developers often work in agile sprints to accelerate product development.

• The system seldom goes down, thanks to robust infrastructure.

• Customers frequently cite ease of use as a reason for choosing our software.

General Facts

• Breakthroughs in computing typically lead to advances in other fields.

• Modern encryption methods ensure secure online transactions.

• Digital marketplaces democratize the sale and distribution of software.

Routines

• A product manager coordinates cross-functional team meetings weekly.

• The marketing team analyzes social media metrics every morning.

• Technicians perform routine maintenance on the cloud servers to prevent downtime.

Answer key p.18

ENGLISH AT THE SPEED OF TECH

UNIT | 01 The Language of Innovation

EXPANSION ACTIVITY: ROLE-PLAY/SIMULATION

In this role-play, you'll simulate a product development meeting focused on planning the scalability of a new prototype. Your conversation should revolve around setting benchmarks, discussing the infrastructure, and the importance of an agile work-flow in the development process. Use the prompts and supporting data to contribute to the discussion and work towards a collaborative action plan. Don't forget to refer back to the Phrase Bank in this lesson as well. A model dialogue is also included for reference.

*TEACHER NOTES: Expansion activities can be more effective when done with a partner, allowing you to practice the language and skills learned in this lesson more fully. If you don't have a teacher, consider practicing with a colleague or friend. Online teachers and tutors are also available at very reasonable rates these days. If you would like teacher notes to support your learning journey, just send an email to **prospeak.author@outlook.com**, and we'll be happy to send you a PDF containing additional task notes, example responses, and expansion activity guidelines.*

ENGLISH AT THE SPEED OF TECH

UNIT 01 The Language of Innovation

Role A

Role: **Product Manager**

Product Scalability Meeting

Background

You are leading the product development meeting. The team has developed an innovative prototype, and you need to guide the conversation towards planning for scalability and establishing clear benchmarks for the next phase. Emphasize the need for agility in the development process.

Prompts

Mention specific benchmarks. Targets call for 99.9% uptime for the product's cloud service and a customer satisfaction score of at least 90%, based on beta-user surveys.

Mention scalability and long-term needs: Include the necessity of upgrading database systems to handle increased user data.

Stress the importance of agility in responding to feedback. Mention that analytics show that responding to user feedback within one development cycle retains 30% more customers.

Mention methods for integrating user feedback. Mention that analytics show that responding to user feedback within one development cycle retains 30% more customers.

NOTES

ENGLISH AT THE SPEED OF TECH

UNIT 01 The Language of Innovation

Role B

Role: Lead Developer

Product Scalability Meeting

Background

As the lead developer, you understand the technical requirements for making the prototype scalable. You're aware of the importance of integrating user feedback and using analytics to guide the product's iterative development.

Prompts

Share insights on technical challenges and potential solutions. Highlight the need to upgrade database systems and move to a more robust cloud solution to handle more user data.

Propose a method for integrating user feedback. Recommend implementing a beta testing phase with select users who can provide ongoing feedback.

Highlight the importance of using analytics. Present user engagement statistics to determine which features should be prioritized.

Discuss the need for a dedicated system to track feedback. Suggest platforms for tracking and analyzing user feedback effectively. Mention that you are looking into some at the moment.

ENGLISH AT THE SPEED OF TECH

UNIT 01 The Language of Innovation

ROLE-PLAY/SIMULATION - SAMPLE DIALOGUE

Alan: Good morning, Yuta. Can we discuss plans for scaling our new prototype? Aiming for 99.9% uptime and a satisfaction score of at least 90% requires us to set benchmarks for cloud services and beta-user feedback.

Yuta: *Hi, Alan. Sure! As scalability targets involve handling lots more user data, we will need to upgrade our database systems and move to a more robust cloud solution.*

Alan: Yes, I agree. We should also propose a method for integrating user feedback into the development process.

Yuta: *Definitely. Integrating real-time data sets will require users who can provide ongoing feedback. We need a dedicated system to track and analyze such data. I'm looking into several platforms now.*

Alan: Thanks, Yuta. We need to keep the process agile, so a solid work-flow is required. Analytics show that responding to user feedback within one development cycle retains 30% more customers.

Yuta: *Absolutely, Alan. We plan on streamlining our feedback loops, establish regular communication with beta testers, and log all suggestions and issues within 24 hours.*

Alan: Sounds great! Before we wrap up, could you briefly highlight how your analysis will guide future product iterations?

Yuta: *Sure. Leveraging analytics to predict trends is key to informing our development. Feedback and testing help us prioritize time spent on specific features requested by users.*

Alan: Perfect! Thanks, Yuta. I'll summarize key points and action items in an email later today. Let's also set up another call for the same time next week.

Expansion - present your own tech concept

Prepare a brief presentation about an innovative technology idea. Use some key vocabulary from this Unit as well as technical terms of your own. Describe your concept, how it works, and its potential impact. Practice presenting your idea aloud, focusing on clear, concise explanations. You can do this alone or with a buddy/teacher for feedback. Aim for a 3-minute presentation that explains your concept to a non-expert audience. This task will help you apply the language skills learned and develop your ability to communicate complex tech ideas simply. Good luck!

KEY VOCABULARY IN CONTEXT

1) The company uses an agile approach for quick adaptation to market shifts.

Incorrect: a) streamline is a verb, not an adjective as is needed here.

Incorrect: c) iterate is a verb, not an adjective.

2) Our new smartwatch prototype uses advanced sensors for increased functionality.

Incorrect: a) disruptive is an adjective, not a noun as is needed here.

Incorrect: c) scalable is an adjective, not a noun.

3) To stay competitive, we must continually innovate and improve our products.

Incorrect: a) agile is an adjective, not a verb as is needed here.

Incorrect: b) analytics is a noun, not a verb.

4) Cloud services provide scalable solutions for most business storage needs.

Incorrect: b) patent is typically a noun or verb, not an adjective as is needed here.

Incorrect: c) streamline is a verb, not an adjective.

5) We set a clear benchmark for energy efficiency that all devices must meet.

Incorrect: a) agile is an adjective, not a noun as is needed here.

Incorrect: b) iterate is a verb, not a noun.

6) The marketing team used advanced analytics to reveal the campaign's success.

Incorrect: b) patent is a noun and unrelated to revealing marketing success.

Incorrect: c) streamline is a verb, not a noun needed here.

7) The legal department is filing a patent for our new battery design.

Incorrect: b) disruptive is an adjective, not a noun as is needed here.

Incorrect: c) innovate is a verb, not a noun.

8) In the tech industry, disruptive innovations rapidly reshape consumer behavior.

Incorrect: a) streamline is a verb, not an adjective as is needed here.

Incorrect: c) analytics is a plural noun, not an adjective.

9) The engineering team plans to iterate on the software for better performance.

Incorrect: b) scalable is an adjective, not a verb as is needed here.

Incorrect: c) disruptive is an adjective, not a verb.

10) The new workflow should streamline our coding processes for improved efficiency.

Incorrect: a) innovative is an adjective, not a verb as is needed here.

Incorrect: b) analytics is a plural noun, not a verb.

ENGLISH AT THE SPEED OF TECH

BUSINESS DIALOGUE COMPREHENSION

Q1: What industry is Alan's team's prototype expected to impact?
• *The prototype is expected to impact the smart-home sector.*

Q2: According to Keiko, why is it important for the design to be scalable?
• *Scalability is important to prepare for initial production and testing.*

Q3: What step does Vikram take to protect their innovation?
• *Vikram has asked Legal to start the patent process to protect their IP.*

Q4: What will Alan do after the meeting today?
• *Alan will send out a summary and next steps in an email and check schedules for a call early next week.*

GRAMMAR PRACTICE

1) He *innovates* new solutions as part of his R&D work.
2) The software *streamlines* the data processing workflow.
3) She *holds* a patent for an eco-friendly battery.
4) It *iterates* through different designs before finalizing.
5) Our company *uses* analytics to understand consumer behavior.
6) They *work* on prototypes until they are complete.
7) The new application *makes* shopping easier for users.
8) She *manages* her team efficiently and effectively.
9) The server *processes* thousands of transactions each second.
10) He attends the annual tech conference every September.

GRAMMAR IN ACTION - PRESENT SIMPLE

Affirmative Statements	Negative Statements	Questions
updates	doesn't compromise	Does... facilitate?
integrate	doesn't overlook	Do... have?
supports	doesn't require	What does... offer?

Frequency	General Facts	Routines
often work	lead to	coordinates
seldom goes	ensure	analyzes
frequently cite	democratize	perform

Unit 01 Notes

....
....
....
....
....
....
....
....

Key takeaways

....
....
....
....

Useful Vocabulary

Use the text boxes below to write the word or phrase on the left and how it was used on the right.

Key words	Example sentence

Useful phrases	Example sentence

ENGLISH AT THE SPEED OF TECH

UNIT 02 Inside the R&D Lab

LEARNING OBJECTIVES

Unit 2 introduces key language and concepts for more effective communication in the R&D space. We learn essential vocabulary and phrases, along with the present continuous tense often used for talking about ongoing projects. 'Inside the R&D Lab' helps you communicate about current projects and innovations, enhancing your role in the fast-paced world of Big Tech. Use this unit to leverage your R&D experience and contribute more effectively to team success - both locally and globally.

Unit 2 Task 1

WARM-UP

Take a minute to think about the questions below. Try to predict what this Unit is going to discuss and how it might benefit your work and your company. Note down your ideas; you will use them as a starting point for our deep dive inside the R&D lab:

- In your own R&D experience, what are some common communication challenges you face?

- How will understanding key R&D vocabulary and trends strengthen your role in the tech sector?

DID YOU KNOW...

"... that Google turned 25 years old on September 27, 2023? Remarkably, the search engine now processes about 8.5 billion searches daily worldwide. Oh, and that you can also thank Jennifer Lopez for Google Images? The US singer's iconic Versace dress, worn at the 2000 Grammy Awards, became Google's most popular search ever at the time, prompting the development of Google Images and evolving the search engine beyond just text-based queries."

UNIT | 02 In the R&D Lab

KEY VOCABULARY IN CONTEXT

precise (adj), specification (n), simulation (n), debug (v), algorithm (n), beta (adj), validate (v), prototyping (n), integration (n), modularity (n)

Read this memo to see the words used in an R&D context.

MEMO

To: Software Development Manager
From: Samson Aliwah, Lead R&D Engineer, TechAdvance Solutions
Date: December 17, 202x
Subject: New AI Language Learning Platform

Dear Prem,

I'm writing to ask your approval for our new project, an AI-Enhanced Language Learning Platform. It's a feature-driven product designed to meet the *precise* needs of the EdTech market.

Please find attached a *specification* that outlines all the important parts of the platform. If approved, we will start the *prototyping* process to set-up an initial *simulation* for testing purposes.

We will be using a unique AI *algorithm* so that first users can test the enhanced learning experience. We will then be using that feedback to *validate* and *debug* the platform to make sure it is working as designed. After that, we hope to move the platform to a *beta* version.

The final testing step in beta will be our *integration* profile. We have designed the platform to work seamlessly with other education technologies based on the platform's *modularity*.

Our R&D team is very positive about this AI project and hope we can work together on some exciting new technology.

Best wishes,

Samson Aliwah
Lead R&D Engineer, TechAdvance Solutions

PRO-TIP: *Look for words you have heard before, but aren't sure about. Try connecting these words to ongoing projects. This method is called 'contextual learning'. Keep a simple 'context journal' on your desk. In it, write where you heard these words and your understanding of how they work. Regularly reviewing this journal will help you remember the words, improving your business English vocabulary in an efficient, practical way.*

ENGLISH AT THE SPEED OF TECH

UNIT 02 In the R&D Lab

KEY VOCABULARY IN CONTEXT - PRACTICE

Complete the sentences below by filling in each blank with the best word from the choices provided. The first one is done for you.

1. We'll . . . . the software's compatibility with automated stress tests.

A. validate	B. scalable	C. analytics

2. Our latest . . . . *streamlines* the software development process.

A. scalable	B. precise	C. specification

3. The . . . . of our new design allows it to work with existing *agile* frameworks.

A. innovate	B. disruptive	C. modularity

4. Our . . . . encourages team members to *innovate* based on feedback.

A. validate	B. prototyping	C. precise

5. The team is working to . . . . the program and maintain its *scalable* architecture.

A. debug	B. simulation	C. disruptive

6. Optimizing the new . . . . has been crucial for our *benchmark* analysis.

A. precise	B. algorithm	C. scalable

7. The . . . . version of our software is being reviewed for *patent* alignment.

A. beta	B. prototyping	C. specification

8. Our engineers are creating . . . . circuit layouts and *iterating* for performance.

A. validate	B. algorithm	C. precise

9. The . . . . of new features ranks well using our latest user analytics.

A. integration	B. precise	C. agile

10. Engineers use . . . . to enhance testing in controlled *virtual* environments.

A. simulations	B. patents	C. precise

Answer key p.31

ENGLISH AT THE SPEED OF TECH

UNIT 02 In the R&D Lab

BUSINESS DIALOGUE

Read the dialogue and answer the comprehension questions that follow below.

Alex: Hey Lisa, I'm running a simulation to test the new algorithm we've developed for the beta version of the app.

Lisa: That's great, Alex. Do the specifications you're using reflect recent design changes?

Alex: Yes, they're updated and precise. I'm debugging the code to make sure everything works smoothly for our demo next week.

Lisa: Good to know. And how is the prototyping going? Are we still maintaining the modularity of our original design?

Alex: Prototyping is on track and the design is highly modular so that integrating with other systems will be much easier.

Lisa: Excellent. Once the simulation is complete, we will need to validate the results to ensure we're ready to move forward.

Alex: Definitely! The validation phase will be critical. I'll compile a report as soon as the simulation data is analyzed.

Lisa: Perfect. After debugging and validation, let's discuss how the algorithm might be improved before the full release.

Alex: Of course. Such iterative improvements are critical. I'll schedule a review of the beta performance based on those goals.

Lisa: Sounds like a plan. Keep me in the loop on the debugging progress and any variations to the specifications that might be required.

Comprehension questions

Q1	What is the main purpose of the simulation Alex is running?
Q2	What does Lisa ask about regarding the design changes?
Q3	Why is modularity important in the design, according to the dialogue?
Q4	What will Alex do after the simulation data is analyzed?

Answer key p.32

ENGLISH AT THE SPEED OF TECH

UNIT | 02 In the R&D Lab

PHRASE BANK

The phrases below should help you to more effectively communicate in R&D lab settings. They cover various aspects of project development, from describing ongoing work to meeting client expectations. Use and practice these phrases to more clearly express your ideas, participate actively in development discussions, and contribute meaningfully to your team's research and development activities.

Describing Ongoing Work
Our team is integrating the ...
I am reviewing the latest ...
We are optimizing the system for ...
Engineers are resolving the current ...

Asking for and Sharing Updates
Could you provide an update on the ...?
I'm planning to send over the ... by ...
QA is expecting the status update by ...
SysAdmin will submit their report by ...

Discussing Technical Challenges
We're addressing some challenges with ...
There are issues arising from the ...
We are dealing with unexpected bugs ...
The team is working through some ...

Offering Solutions
I suggest implementing ...
Let's consider adopting ...
I recommend revising ...
Perhaps we should explore ...

Collaborating with Teams
We are coordinating with the ... team for ...
I am working with our engineers on ...
Our cross-functional efforts are leading to ...
We are joining forces with CS to ...

Planning for Scalability
The... is designed with scalability in mind.
We need to ensure the ... is capable of ...
Our scalability strategy involves ...
We are upgrading (the) ... in order to. ..

Discussing Benchmarks
Our goal is achieving ...
We are aiming for ...
Let's set the benchmark at ... for ...
Our... benchmark should be based on ...

Emphasizing Agility
We must stay agile in ... so we can ...
Our team is adapting rapidly to ...
We are streamlining ... in order to ...
Staying agile means being ready to ...

Troubleshooting Issues
We're working non-stop to identify ...
Our immediate focus is on fixing ...
We are mapping out a plan to tackle ...
The team is dedicated to resolving ...

Meeting Client Expectations
The client is expecting ... by ...
Project specs must align with the client's ...
Client satisfaction is our top priority as we ...
Our... is designed to match the client's ...

CULTURE TIP

"Effective communication is key to successful global R&D. Actively listening to others, while expressing your own ideas simply and clearly helps foster teamwork and collaboration. Promoting open discussions where everyone feels comfortable and shares thoughts and ideas is also essential. This approach not only enhances problem-solving but helps to bridge cultural differences, leading to more effective business solutions."

ENGLISH AT THE SPEED OF TECH

UNIT 02 In the R&D Lab

GRAMMAR FOCUS: PRESENT CONTINUOUS

The present continuous tense is often used to talk about ongoing projects. The tense is formed with the verb 'to be' (am, is, are) followed by the '-ing' form of the main verb. The present continuous tense allows you to convey actions that are currently happening or plans that are in progress, which is particularly useful in the dynamic R&D environment where projects evolve rapidly.

1. We are testing the new interface for any usability issues.

2. Our team is developing a prototype that integrates the latest AI technology.

3. We are working with the cybersecurity team to enhance data-protection protocols.

4. The engineers are working on refining the code to improve system efficiency.

5. Our department is focusing on streamlining the product-development process.

Tip: Use the present continuous tense as if you're giving a live update on a project or event. Just like live reporting on the news, it allows you to express actions as they're happening. This method helps you to associate the tense with activities that are active and ongoing. For example, when you need to report "Our team is integrating the new live-streaming protocol," think of it as narrating the immediate action, like a reporter covering an event. This 'live narration' technique will remind you to use the present continuous tense for real-time project updates.

Unit 2 Task 5

GRAMMAR PRACTICE

Change the verbs in the following sentences from their base form to the present continuous tense. Remember to think about the situation as if you're giving a live update on a project or event and expressing actions as they're happening.

1. He . . . . (innovate) new solutions to overcome the technical challenges.

2. She . . . . (develop) a cutting-edge algorithm to enhance data processing.

3. They . . . . (test) the prototype's durability under extreme conditions.

4. I . . . . (examine) the latest data analytics for market trends.

5. We . . . . (design) a user-friendly interface to improve customer experience.

6. You . . . . (refine) the software code to optimize its performance.

7. We . . . . (integrate) advanced features to stay ahead in the tech market.

8. He . . . . (explore) different modularity options for the new software platform.

9. I . . . . (conduct) a series of simulations to predict product behavior.

10. They . . . . (assess) the system's scalability to support future growth.

Answer key p.32

ENGLISH AT THE SPEED OF TECH

UNIT 02 In the R&D Lab

GRAMMAR IN ACTION: PROJECT UPDATE EMAIL

Compose an email update about an ongoing project using the present continuous tense, then check your email with the model answer.

Scenario: You are a key member of the "SafeNet App" development team, tasked with improving online security through a mobile application. Draft an email to your supervisor detailing the latest project developments. You need to report on:

- *The programming team's engagement with the encryption algorithms.*
- *Progress being made by the UI/UX designers on the new user interface.*
- *Your collaborative efforts with the marketing team for the upcoming launch.*
- *The QA team's process of testing the app and troubleshooting issues.*

Email guidelines: *Introduction*: Briefly state the purpose of the email. *Body*: Provide a detailed update on the points above using the present continuous tense. *Conclusion*: Sum up the current status and next steps. *Self-Checking:* After writing your email, compare it to a provided model answer to evaluate your use of the present continuous tense and how well you covered the required points.

Subject: ....

....

....

....

....

....

....

....

....

Answer key p.32

ENGLISH AT THE SPEED OF TECH

UNIT | 02 In the R&D Lab

EXPANSION ACTIVITY: ROLE-PLAY/SIMULATION

In this role-play, you'll simulate a meeting to address an unexpected technical setback with a new software feature. Your dialogue should revolve around diagnosing the issue, proposing immediate actions, and planning the next steps to ensure the project remains on track. Use the prompts and supporting data to contribute to the discussion and work towards a collaborative solution. Don't forget to refer back to the Phrase Bank in this lesson as well. A model dialogue is also included for reference.

*TEACHER NOTES: Expansion activities can be more effective when done with a partner, allowing you to practice the language and skills learned in this lesson more fully. If you don't have a teacher, consider practicing with a colleague or friend. Online teachers and tutors are also available at very reasonable rates these days. If you would like teacher notes to support your learning journey, just send an email to **prospeak.author@outlook.com**, and we'll be happy to send you a PDF containing additional task notes, example responses, and expansion activity guidelines.*

ENGLISH AT THE SPEED OF TECH

Role A
Role: **R&D Manager**

Addressing a Technical Setback

Background

You are the R&D Manager in a meeting to discuss an unexpected technical setback with a new software feature. The feature is crucial for the next update, and the team is under pressure to resolve the issue promptly. Your goal is to lead the team in a problem-solving discussion, making sure to cover all technical aspects while also considering the impact on the project time line.

Prompts

Outline the situation: Begin by summarizing the technical setback and its implications for the project.

Establish urgency: Emphasize the importance of resolving the issue quickly due to the upcoming client demo.

Call for insights: Ask for thoughts on potential causes of the problem.

Encourage collaboration: Suggest working together to brainstorm possible solutions and emphasize the need to collaborate with other teams.

Emphasize the time line: Remind the team of the project milestones and inquire about realistic time frames for troubleshooting and implementing fixes.

NOTES

ENGLISH AT THE SPEED OF TECH

UNIT 02 In the R&D Lab

Role B

Role: Lead Software Developer

Addressing a Technical Setback

Background

As the Lead Software Developer, you're directly responsible for the technical direction of the software project. You're aware that the recent integration of a third-party API for enhanced user authentication might be conflicting with the existing encryption algorithms, leading to the current instability. With the client demo looming, you understand the pressure to not only fix the issue but also to ensure that the overall project time line remains on track.

Prompts

Acknowledge the problem: Confirm your awareness of the system instability issue and the ongoing efforts to resolve it.

Share technical insights: Discuss the diagnostics you are running and the code revisions you are examining to pinpoint the source of the bug.

Suggest immediate actions: Offer a brief overview of the solutions you are considering to address the bug without compromising the project's overall progress.

Estimate a realistic time line: Provide an informed estimate of how quickly you are implementing fixes and when a stable version will be ready for retesting.

Confirm your commitment: Reassure the R&D Manager that you are dedicating the necessary resources and expertise to overcome this setback while upholding the quality and security standards expected by the client.

ENGLISH AT THE SPEED OF TECH

ROLE-PLAY/SIMULATION - SAMPLE DIALOGUE

Jordan: Good morning, Alex. Our team is integrating the new software feature, but we've encountered a technical setback that is impacting our project time line.

Alex: *Hi, Jordan. Yes, I'm reviewing the latest diagnostics and am aware of the instability issues. We suspect it might be due to the new API integration.*

Jordan: This issue needs our immediate attention. Could you provide an update on the potential causes?

Alex: *Preliminary diagnostics point to conflicts between the API and our encryption algorithms.*

Jordan: Let's brainstorm some solutions. Can you suggest any immediate actions to mitigate the compatibility issues?

Alex: *I propose isolating the affected modules and revising the code to ensure compatibility.*

Jordan: Our upcoming client demo means time is of the essence here. Can you give me a realistic time-frame for implementing those fixes?

Alex: *I believe we can have a stable version ready for retesting in three days.*

Jordan: Collaboration with developers and QA is key here. How are you coordinating with other teams on this?

Alex: *I'm working closely with the front-end and QA teams to align our fixes with the client's specifications.*

Jordan: Excellent. We all need to remember that meeting client expectations is paramount. Please keep me updated on progress.

Alex: *Absolutely, Jordan. We're committed to resolving this issue swiftly and maintaining the quality standards expected by our client.*

Expansion - Prepare Your Own R&D Project Update

Give a brief presentation on the current status of an R&D project you are involved in, or imagine a realistic one. Use key vocabulary from this unit, along with any relevant technical terms you know. Detail the project's current development stage, ongoing challenges, and strategies being implemented. Practice delivering this update aloud, ensuring your explanation is clear and concise. This can be done individually or with a partner/teacher for constructive feedback. Aim for a presentation length of about 3 minutes, tailored for listeners who may not have a technical background. This exercise will assist you in applying the language skills acquired to effectively communicate the details of an R&D project in a clear and simplified manner. Good luck!"

ENGLISH AT THE SPEED OF TECH

UNIT | 02 Answer Key

KEY VOCABULARY IN CONTEXT

1) We'll validate the software's *compatibility* **with automated stress tests.**
Incorrect: b) scalable is an adjective, not a verb as is needed here.
Incorrect: c) analytics is a plural noun, not a verb.

2) Our latest specification *streamlines* **the software development process.**
Incorrect: a) scalable is an adjective, not a noun as is needed here.
Incorrect: b) precise is an adjective, not a noun.

3) The modularity of our new design allows it to work with existing *agile* **frameworks.**
Incorrect: a) innovate is a verb, not a noun as is needed here.
Incorrect: b) disruptive is an adjective, not a noun.

4) Our prototyping encourages team members to *innovate* **based on feedback.**
Incorrect: a) validate is a verb, not a noun as is needed here.
Incorrect: c) precise is an adjective, not a noun.

5) The team is working to debug the program and maintain its *scalable* **architecture.**
Incorrect: b) simulation is a noun, not a verb that needed here.
Incorrect: c) disruptive is an adjective, not a verb.

6) Optimizing the new algorithm has been crucial for our *benchmark* **analysis.**
Incorrect: a) precise is an adjective, not a noun as is needed here.
Incorrect: c) scalable is an adjective, not a noun.

7) The beta version of our software is being reviewed for *patent* **alignment.**
Incorrect: b) prototyping is a present participle, but does not generally modify 'version'.
Incorrect: c) specification is a noun, not an adjective as is needed here.

8) Our engineers are creating precise circuit layouts and *iterating* **for performance.**
Incorrect: a) validate is a verb, not an adjective as is needed here.
Incorrect: b) algorithm is a noun, not an adjective.

9) The integration of new features ranks well using our latest user *analytics.*
Incorrect: b) precise is an adjective, not a noun as is needed here.
Incorrect: c) agile (method) is an adjective, not a noun.

10) Engineers use simulations to enhance testing in controlled *virtual* **environments.**
Incorrect: b) patents focus on legal protection, not testing or development.
Incorrect: c) precise is an adjective, not a noun as is needed here.

NOTE: words in sentences 1-10 in *italics* are spaced repetition key words from previous units.

ENGLISH AT THE SPEED OF TECH

UNIT 02 Answer Key

BUSINESS DIALOGUE COMPREHENSION

Q1: What is the main purpose of the simulation Alex is running?
• *To test the new algorithm developed for the beta version of the app.*
Rationale: In the first line, Alex states he is running a simulation for this specific purpose.

Q2: What does Lisa ask about regarding the design changes?
• *Lisa asks if the specifications Alex is using reflect the recent design changes.*
Rationale: Lisa's first turn in the dialogue shows her concern.

Q3: Why is modularity important in the design, according to the dialogue?
• *Because it will make integrating the design with other systems much easier.*
Rationale: Alex mentions that the design's high modularity is on track, which implies that this feature is key for future integration flexibility.

Q4: What will Alex do after the simulation data is analyzed?
• *Alex will compile a report as soon as he has analyzed the simulation data.*
Rationale: Alex confirms next steps in response to Lisa's comment about moving forward after the simulation is completed.

GRAMMAR PRACTICE

1) He *is innovating* new solutions to overcome the technical challenges.
2) She *is developing* a cutting-edge algorithm to enhance data processing.
3) They *are testing* the prototype's durability under extreme conditions.
4) I *am examining* the latest data analytics for market trends.
5) We *are designing* a user-friendly interface to improve customer experience.
6) You *are refining* the software code to optimize its performance.
7) We *are integrating* advanced features to stay ahead in the tech market.
8) He *is exploring* different modularity options for the new software platform.
9) I *am conducting* a series of simulations to predict product behavior.
10) They *are assessing* the system's scalability to support future growth.

GRAMMAR IN ACTION: PROJECT UPDATE EMAIL

Example model answer:
Subject: Update on the Online Security App Development
Hi Robin,

I hope this email finds you well. I***'m writing*** to provide you with the latest developments in the online security application project.

Currently, our programming team i**s integrating** advanced encryption features to enhance security measures. In parallel, the UI/UX design team *is making progress* on the new user interface, *aiming to* balance aesthetics with user-friendliness. We've hit a few snags, but *are actively collaborating* with the design team to iron them out.

On the promotional front, I *am working closely* with the marketing department, which *is conducting* preliminary market research to inform our launch strategy.

In terms of quality assurance, the QA team *is testing* app features and *is also troubleshooting* any issues as they arise, *ensuring* we adhere to our high standards.

Thank you for your ongoing support. I will be sure to keep you updated on our progress and any new developments.

Best regards,

Unit 02 Notes

....

....

....

....

....

....

....

....

Key takeaways

....

....

....

....

Useful Vocabulary

Use the text boxes below to write the word or phrase on the left and how it was used on the right.

Key words	Example sentence

Useful phrases	Example sentence

ENGLISH AT THE SPEED OF TECH

UNIT | 03 Tech Support and Customer Service

LEARNING OBJECTIVES

Welcome to Unit 3: Tech Support and Customer Service. In this lesson, you will learn essential language and skills for more effective tech support, including a review of the past simple tense to talk about incident reports. Learn to resolve problems through real-world tech support scenarios, and enhance your ability to communicate solutions more effectively in the technical support and customer service fields. Develop skills in handling technical calls and crafting professional follow-up emails that are critical for executing exceptional customer service in the tech industry.

WARM-UP

Take a moment to consider the questions below. Reflect on what you think this unit will cover and how it could be beneficial in your role in tech support and customer service. Make a note of your thoughts so you can refer to them later; these ideas will help your exploration into Tech Support and Customer Service:

- What common challenges do you encounter when handling tech support calls?
- How might improved communication skills enhance your effectiveness in customer service in the tech arena?

DID YOU KNOW...

"... that even small improvements in customer retention can significantly boost company profits, sometimes by as much as 25%? Most customers are likely to spend more after a positive service experience, while a single negative experience can lead them to consider leaving. Focusing on good customer service truly contributes to business success. Not only does it reduce marketing costs and increase revenue through repeat business, but satisfied customers are also more likely to recommend the company to others, driving growth even further."

Unit 3 Task 2

KEY VOCABULARY IN CONTEXT

clarify (v), diagnostic (adj), solution (n), escalate (v), firmware (n), helpful (adj), assistance (n), update (n), ticket (n), responsive (adj)

Read the proposal from Miki Shorer to see the words used in a Tech and Customer support context.

Proposal: Optimizing Tech Support and Customer Service

To: Senior Management
From: Miki Shorer, Manager, Tech Support and Customer Service

Introduction

After several meetings with my team, I am pleased to propose improvements to our Tech Support and Customer Service processes. The team has worked hard to find ideas that will improve our services, help customers, and answer calls more efficiently. These changes will help us keep our promise of 'best in class' customer *assistance*.

Key Changes

Improved Diagnostic Tools:

We are planning to implement better *diagnostic* tools to *clarify* customer problems. This will help us find the right *solutions* in a more timely manner.

Updating Firmware and Managing Tickets:

We will regularly *update* our *firmware* to avoid technical problems. We also want to make our *ticket* processing system more *responsive* so we can provide quicker assistance to our customers.

Clear Escalation Rules and Additional Training:

We will make clear rules for when to *escalate* difficult issues. We will also train our staff more so they be more responsive and effective when helping customers.

Conclusion

By making these changes, we can improve how we support our customers. Our team will then be more responsive and ready to offer *helpful* and timely assistance.

Best regards,
Miki Shorer
Manager, Tech Support and Customer Service

PRO-TIP: *Try some 'lexical mapping' by connecting new vocabulary to areas like troubleshooting, client support, or system diagnostics. Create a visual map with these words, drawing connections to common support scenarios or customer queries. This method will help you understand how these terms are interconnected and directly applicable to your daily tasks in tech support and customer service.*

ENGLISH AT THE SPEED OF TECH

UNIT | 03 Tech Support and Customer Service

Unit 3 Task 3   KEY VOCABULARY IN CONTEXT - PRACTICE

Complete the sentences below by filling in each blank with the best word from the choices provided. The first one is done for you.

1. To . . . . the problem, we used a *prototype* for more accurate results.

A. benchmarking	**B. clarify**	C. innovative

2. Our . . . . approach addressed the *scalable* nature of our support system.

A. diagnostic	B. streamlining	C. disrupted

3. The best . . . . for network issues was *streamlining* our responses.

A. solution	B. innovating	C. iterates

4. We . . . . the call to a senior technician if the *debug* process fails.

A. scalability	B. escalate	C. modular

5. Updating the . . . . to v2.1 increased the software's *modularity*.

A. benchmarking	B. firmware	C. innovative

6. Providing . . . . tech support meant *agile* solutions to complex problems.

A. disruptive	B. algorithm	C. helpful

7. . . . . with browser access often required checking *benchmark* performance data.

A. Assistance	B. Scalable	C. Algorithm

8. We regularly . . . . our system to include the latest customer support *analytics*.

A. innovation	B. streamlines	C. updated

9. Each support . . . . was a unique opportunity to provide *innovative* solutions.

A. scalability	B. ticket	C. validated

10. Our . . . . approach involved *iterating* based on customer support data.

A. algorithm	B. modularity	C. responsive

Answer key p.45

36

ENGLISH AT THE SPEED OF TECH

UNIT | 03 Tech Support and Customer Service

BUSINESS DIALOGUE

Read the dialogue and answer the comprehension questions that follow below.

Vivek: Hi Sara, I read your technical brief on Customer Service. Can you clarify a bit more about the improved diagnostic tools?

Sara: Sure. We updated the tools to more accurately identify customer issues. This change alone improved our efficiency a lot.

Vivek: Sounds promising. And how about the firmware updates? Were they responsive to the recent technical issues?

Sara: Yes, they not only fixed those problems but also helped with some performance gains.

Vivek: Great to hear. Now, about the ticketing system - did the new updates make it easier for customers to input queries?

Sara: Yes. The system is now far more responsive. We've seen a noticeable improvement in resolutions and customer satisfaction.

Vivek: Great! I heard we completed some recent training to reduce the need for escalating issues. How did the team respond to the online format?

Sara: Overall, feedback was very positive and the team has adapted well. We are now more responsive when handling complex customer issues.

Vivek: That's excellent, Sara. Please keep me updated on further progress. It's essential we maintain high standards in our customer support.

Sara: Will do. I'm confident these changes have set us on the right path to enhance the customer service experience even further.

Comprehension questions

Q1   What was the main purpose of updating the diagnostic tools, according to Sara?

Q2   How did the firmware updates impact the system's performance?

Q3   What improvement was observed in the ticketing system after the updates?

Q4   How did the team respond to the recent training and its online format?

Answer key p.46

ENGLISH AT THE SPEED OF TECH

UNIT | 03 Tech Support and Customer Service

PHRASE BANK

The phrases below will assist your communication in tech support and customer service roles. They cover a range of situations, from handling customer queries to reflecting on experiences. Use these phrases to articulate your responses effectively, engage confidently in support scenarios, and deliver outstanding customer service to internal and external stakeholders.

Handling Customer Queries
The CS team addressed ... promptly.
Tech support clarified ... with the client.
We offered timely assistance with ...
We responded to ... and ...

Describing Technical Issues
The problem occurred due to ...
We have identified ...
The system is experiencing a ...
The issue appears to be ...

Explaining Diagnostic Steps
We checked ... for errors.
Technicians ran ... on the system.
I inspected ... for faults.
We evaluated the ...

Proposing Solutions
I suggest upgrading ...
We recommend installing ...
It would best to reduce ...
We should implement ...

Providing Updates and Feedback
The team updated ... to resolve ...
We resolved the issue through ...
I improved ... with the latest ...
Users noted increased ... after ...

Managing Tickets and Requests
The team opened a ticket for ...
Tech support assigned tickets to ...
We prioritized the ticket for ...
I closed the ticket after ...

Discussing Preventative Measures
We plan to implement regular ...
Let's schedule ongoing ...
Our strategy includes ...
The team will train staff on ...

Reporting and Documenting
The support team documented ...
Our report detailed ...
We compiled a report on ...
We recorded changes made to ...

Communicating with Team Members
We coordinated with ... for ...
We discussed ... with the team.
We updated the team on ...
The team shared insights from ...

Reflecting on Experiences
We reviewed ... and learned...
We applied lessons from ...
Our review improved ... based on ...
The team reviewed ... to avoid ...

CULTURE TIP

"In customer service situations, excellent listening skills and clear communication are key. Thoroughly understanding customer issues and explaining solutions simply and effectively not only resolves problems efficiently but also builds customer trust and satisfaction in a global tech environment."

ENGLISH AT THE SPEED OF TECH

UNIT | 03 Tech Support and Customer Service

GRAMMAR FOCUS: PAST SIMPLE

The past simple tense is often used to describe completed actions or resolved issues, such as in 'The update worked' or 'We patched the bug.' This tense allows for clear communication about past events, which is crucial for talking about technical problems. Its straightforward structure aids effective dialogue between customers and support personnel, making it a key grammar point for support and service interactions.

1. We **received** your complaint about the app and fixed the bug immediately.

2. Our technician **repaired** the faulty battery on the device this morning.

3. We successfully **upgraded** the server to improve performance.

4. I **checked** the network settings and found the source of the issue.

5. A user **reported** a glitch this morning, which we are working to address.

Tip: The 'When-What-Why' Rule for Past Simple
When for Time: Use the past simple to indicate *when* an action happened in the past.
For example: "I updated the software yesterday."
What for Actions: Use the past simple to describe *what* action was completed.
For example: "The team solved the technical issue."
Why for Reasons: Use it to explain *why* something was done.
For example: "We changed the password for security reasons."

Unit 3 Task 5

GRAMMAR PRACTICE

Using the *When/Time-What/Action-Why/Reason* rule for past simple tense, look at the sentences below and decide which one of the three apply and then underline the relevant part of the sentence. The first one is done for you.

1. (When/Time) Our development team successfully upgraded the server <u>last week</u>.

2. (. . . . .) The system crashed due to a faulty power source.

3. (. . . . .) Our team resolved the connectivity issue earlier this morning.

4. (. . . . .) I completed the project's data analysis as requested.

5. (. . . . .) We changed our software provider to enhance security.

6. (. . . . .) Another customer called about the login problem this morning.

7. (. . . . .) We fixed the critical bug to prevent any potential data loss.

8. (. . . . .) Our manager reviewed the project plan we submitted.

9. (. . . . .) We relocated the server room due to overheating issues.

10. (. . . . .) The new app was launched last month to assist clients.

Answer key p.46

ENGLISH AT THE SPEED OF TECH

UNIT | 03 Tech Support and Customer Service

GRAMMAR IN ACTION: INCIDENT REPORT

Write a brief incident report about resolving a network connectivity issue with an internal team that experienced recurring problems with network connectivity, impacting their work. You should include:

- **Issue Description:** *Briefly describe the network connectivity problems.*
- **Initial Assessment:** *Detail the first steps in diagnosing the issue.*
- **Actions Taken:** *Explain the specific actions you undertook to resolve the problem (e.g., hardware checks, software updates, configuration changes).*
- **Outcome:** *Describe the results of your actions, including restored network functionality.*
- **Preventative Measures:** *Mention any steps taken to prevent future occurrences.*
- **Team Feedback:** *Include any feedback or results observed by the sales team post-resolution.*

Incident Report: Network Connectivity Issue Resolution ....

Issue Description: ....

....

Initial Assessment: ....

....

Actions Taken: ....

....

....

Outcome: ....

....

Preventative Measures: ....

....

....

Team Feedback: ....

....

Answer key p.46

ENGLISH AT THE SPEED OF TECH

UNIT | 03 Tech Support and Customer Service

EXPANSION ACTIVITY: ROLE-PLAY/SIMULATION

In this role-play, you'll simulate a meeting between a Tech Support Specialist and the manager of a department that recently experienced a network connectivity issue. Your conversation will focus on identifying the problem, discussing the steps taken to resolve it, and exploring preventative measures for the future. Utilize the provided prompts to guide your dialogue, ensuring to incorporate the past simple tense to reflect on the actions taken last week. Refer back to the Phrase Bank from this lesson to effectively communicate technical aspects and responses. This exercise aims to develop a practical understanding of resolving tech support issues within a collaborative framework. A model dialogue is also included for reference.

*TEACHER NOTES: Expansion activities can be more effective when done with a partner, allowing you to practice the language and skills learned in this lesson more fully. If you don't have a teacher, consider practicing with a colleague or friend. Online teachers and tutors are also available at very reasonable rates these days. If you would like teacher notes to support your learning journey, just send an email to **prospeak.author@outlook.com**, and we'll be happy to send you a PDF containing additional task notes, example responses, and expansion activity guidelines.*

ENGLISH AT THE SPEED OF TECH

UNIT 03 Tech Support and Customer Service

Role A
Role: Tech Support Specialist

Internal Tech Support Query

Background

You are a Tech Support Specialist who recently resolved a significant network issue. The problem was initially reported through an internal ticketing system by an employee, indicating connectivity problems impacting their department's work. Today, you're in a follow-up virtual meeting with the department manager to review the incident, ensuring all concerns have been addressed and to discuss any lessons learned from the experience.

Prompts

Summarize the Issue: Start by summarizing the network issue and acknowledge its impact on the affected department.

Discuss Diagnostic Steps: Explain the steps taken to diagnose the issue, such as checking server logs or inspecting hardware.

Describe Resolution Process: Detail the actions followed to address the problem, like updating software or adjusting firmware settings.

Provide Reassurance: Offer reassurance and mention that similar issues were resolved in the past.

Discuss Preventative Measures: Explain the measures in place to prevent similar issues in the future.

NOTES

ENGLISH AT THE SPEED OF TECH

UNIT 03 Tech Support and Customer Service

NOTES

_____

....

....

....

....

....

....

....

Role B	Role: **Department Manager**
Internal Tech Support Query	

Background

You are the manager of the department that experienced recent network connectivity problems. After raising the initial ticket last week, you are now in a scheduled virtual follow-up meeting with the Tech Support Specialist. The purpose is to provide feedback on the resolution, discuss any ongoing concerns, and ensure that effective measures are in place to prevent future occurrences.

Prompts

Acknowledge the Summary: Confirm the summary of the issue and its impact on work.

Ask about Resolution Steps: Inquire about the specific steps taken to resolve the issue.

React to Resolution: Provide feedback on the effectiveness of the solution implemented.

Inquire about Prevention: Ask about measures to prevent such issues in the future.

Give Feedback on Communication: Provide feedback on the effectiveness of communication during the incident.

ENGLISH AT THE SPEED OF TECH

UNIT 03 Tech Support and Customer Service

ROLE-PLAY/SIMULATION - SAMPLE DIALOGUE

Alec: Hi Jordan, The purpose of this call is to follow-up on your network issues last week. To summarize, you had problems that affected your team's access to cloud storage and client communications. Is that correct?

Jordan: *That's right, Alec. The network outage really impacted our work and we were offline for hours.*

Alec: I see. When we first looked into it, we checked the server logs and found some errors. Technicians then ran system diagnostics and inspected the hardware for faults.

Jordan: *That sounds thorough. What exactly did you find?*

Alec: We traced it to a firmware issue, so we ran a patch to resolve the problem. Additionally, we adjusted some settings to improve system stability.

Jordan: *I see. The solution was effective and seems to be stable, but how confident are you that this won't happen again?*

Alec: Very confident. We've resolved similar issues in the past and have implemented measures to prevent future occurrences. We're also monitoring the network more closely to catch potential issues early.

Jordan: *Great to hear. The last time something like this happened, the communication wasn't great. I appreciate you keeping us in the loop this time.*

Alec: Absolutely, Jordan. Keeping you informed is a priority. If you experience any further issues, don't hesitate to reach out immediately.

Jordan: *Will do, Alec. Thanks again for addressing this so quickly. Hopefully, we won't have a repeat of last week's chaos.*

Alec: You're welcome, Jordan. I'm here to ensure everything runs smoothly and the team will stay proactive to keep the network reliable.

Expansion - Prepare a proposal

Outline potential improvements to your company's Tech Support and Customer Service department. Use key vocabulary from this Unit, along with any relevant technical terms and phrases. Describe specific enhancements such as new training initiatives, technology updates, or work-flow modifications. Practice presenting your proposal aloud, ensuring your communication is clear and persuasive. This can be done individually or with a partner/ teacher for constructive feedback. Aim for a presentation length of about 3 minutes, focusing on presenting your ideas in a way that is accessible to a non-technical audience. This exercise will help you apply the language skills acquired to effectively communicate customer service improvement strategies in a professional setting. Good luck!

KEY VOCABULARY IN CONTEXT

1) To clarify the problem, we used a *prototype* for more accurate results.

Incorrect: a) benchmarking is a gerund form, not a base verb as is needed here.

Incorrect: c) innovative is an adjective, not a verb.

2) Our diagnostic approach addressed the *scalable* nature of our support system.

Incorrect: b) streamlining is a gerund verb, not an adjective as is needed here.

Incorrect: c) disrupted is a past tense verb, not typically used as an adjective.

3) The best solution for network issues was *streamlining* our responses.

Incorrect: b) innovating is a gerund form, not a standard noun as is needed here.

Incorrect: c) iterates is a verb, not a noun.

4) We escalate the call to a senior technician if the *debug* process fails.

Incorrect: a) scalability is a noun, not a verb as is needed here.

Incorrect: c) modular is an adjective, not a verb.

5) Updating the firmware to v2.1 increased the software's *modularity*.

Incorrect: a) benchmarking is a gerund form, not a standard noun as is needed here.

Incorrect: c) innovative is an adjective, not a noun.

6) Providing helpful tech support meant *agile* solutions to complex problems.

Incorrect: b) algorithm is a noun, not an adjective as is needed here.

Incorrect: a) disruptive is an adjective, but does not fit this context.

7) Assistance with browser access often required checking *benchmark* performance data.

Incorrect: b) scalable is an adjective, not a noun as is needed here.

Incorrect: c) algorithm is a noun, but does not fit this context.

8) We regularly updated our system to include the latest customer support *analytics*

Incorrect: a) innovation is a noun, not a verb as is needed here.

Incorrect: b) streamlines does not fit with the subject 'we'.

9) Each support ticket was a unique opportunity to provide *innovative* solutions.

Incorrect: a) scalability is a noun, but does not fit this context.

Incorrect: c) validated is a past tense verb, not a noun as is needed here.

10) Our responsive approach involved *iterating* based on customer support data.

Incorrect: b) modularity is a noun, not an adjective as is needed here.

Incorrect: a) algorithm is a noun, not an adjective.

NOTE: words in sentences 1-10 in ***italics*** are spaced repetition key words from previous units.

ENGLISH AT THE SPEED OF TECH

Unit 3 Task 4 ## BUSINESS DIALOGUE COMPREHENSION

Q1: What was the main purpose of updating the diagnostic tools, according to Sara?
- *To more accurately identify customer issues.*
Rationale: Sara states that the update aimed to improve issue identification.

Q2: How did the firmware updates impact the system's performance?
- *They fixed problems and enhanced performance.*
Rationale: Sara confirms the updates improved the system's modularity and performance.

Q3: What improvement was observed in the ticket system after the updates?
- *It became more responsive and improved customer satisfaction.*
Rationale: Sara notes the ticket system's increased responsiveness and improved resolutions.

Q4: How did the team respond to the recent training and its online format?
- *The team adapted well and improved in handling complex issues.*
Rationale: Sara remarks on the team's positive adaptation to the new training format.

Unit 3 Task 5 ## GRAMMAR PRACTICE

1) *(When/Time):* Our tech team successfully upgraded the server <u>last week</u>.

2) *(What/Action):* The <u>system crashed</u> due to a faulty power source.

3) *(When/Time):* Our team resolved the connectivity issue earlier <u>this morning</u>.

4) *(What/Action):* I <u>completed the</u> project's <u>data analysis</u> as requested.

5) *(Why/Reason):* We changed our software provider <u>to enhance security</u>.

6) *(When/Time):* Another customer called about the login problem <u>this morning</u>.

7) *(Why/Reason):* We fixed the critical bug <u>to prevent</u> any potential <u>data loss</u>.

8) *(What/Action):* Our manager <u>reviewed the project plan</u> we submitted.

9) *(Why/Reason):* We relocated the server room <u>due to overheating</u> issues.

10) *(When/Time):* The new app was launched <u>last month </u>to assist clients.

Unit 3 Task 6 ## GRAMMAR IN ACTION: INCIDENT REPORT

Example model answer:

Incident Report: Network Connectivity Issue Resolution

Issue Description: The sales team has <u>experienced</u> frequent network connectivity problems. These ranged from slow internet speeds to complete loss of access, hindering their ability to manage sales orders.

Initial Assessment: Upon notification, I began systematic network checks. I <u>reviewed</u> logs and <u>monitored</u> connectivity status to pinpoint any irregular patterns or disruptions.

Actions Taken: *Hardware:* <u>Inspected</u> routers and switches for any faults. <u>Found</u> no hardware issues. *Software:* <u>Updated</u> the network drivers and firmware to the latest versions.

Config Changes: <u>Optimized</u> network settings for performance and <u>reduced</u> bottlenecks.

Outcome: The connectivity issues were resolved after the updates and configuration adjustments. The sales team <u>reported</u> a stable and faster network connection, with no disruptions <u>observed</u> in the following days.

Preventative Measures: <u>Implemented</u> regular network maintenance checks and <u>scheduled</u> automatic updates for network software to minimize future connectivity problems.

Team Feedback: The sales team <u>expressed</u> relief and satisfaction with the <u>restored</u> network functionality. They <u>reported</u> an improvement in communication efficiency with clients and smoother handling of sales orders.

Unit 03 Notes

....
....
....
....
....
....
....
....

Key takeaways

....
....
....
....

Useful Vocabulary

Use the text boxes below to write the word or phrase on the left and how it was used on the right.

Key words	Example sentence

Useful phrases	Example sentence

ENGLISH AT THE SPEED OF TECH

UNIT | 04 Cybersecurity Essentials

LEARNING OBJECTIVES

Welcome to Unit 4: Cybersecurity Essentials. In this lesson, you will practice the key language of cybersecurity in the tech sector, using the future simple tense to discuss anticipated security measures and upcoming challenges. This unit guides you through practical cybersecurity scenarios, enhancing your ability to more effectively communicate strategies and responses to digital threats. Develop skills in identifying security risks, discussing preventative strategies, and articulating key cybersecurity concepts— essential for maintaining high security standards in the rapidly evolving landscape of Big Tech.

Unit 4 Task 1

WARM-UP

Before moving on with this unit, let's direct your focus towards cybersecurity in the tech sector. Consider these questions and note down your ideas. They will provide some scaffolding for your exploration of Cybersecurity Essentials in this lesson:

- How does cybersecurity impact your daily tasks in the tech industry?
- Read the paragraph below and think about another cybersecurity trend or fact that recently caught your attention.

DID YOU KNOW...

"... cybersecurity teams now harness AI not only for defensive purposes but also to predict cyber attacks? AI systems can analyze data to uncover hacker patterns undetectable to humans. These advanced algorithms foresee cyber threats by identifying unusual network behavior, helping to stay one step ahead of cybercriminals. This shift in approach is revolutionizing how Big Tech tackles cybersecurity challenges. As AI continues to evolve, its role in cybersecurity will likely expand, offering even more sophisticated defences against emerging threats."

ENGLISH AT THE SPEED OF TECH

UNIT | 04 Cybersecurity Essentials

KEY VOCABULARY IN CONTEXT

encrypt (v), firewall (n), confidential (adj), monitor (v), malware (n), vulnerability (n), compliance (n), protect (v), patch (n), secure (adj)

Read this email to see the words used in a Cybersecurity context.

Subject: Enhanced Cybersecurity Measures

Dear Colleagues,

I am writing to inform you of the recent enhancements to our company-wide cybersecurity measures. To *protect* our network, we have implemented a comprehensive *firewall*, critical to defending against digital threats. This is part of our ongoing effort to ensure all *confidential* data remains *secure*.

In our commitment to robust cybersecurity, we now *monitor* systems continuously for *malware*, a first step in identifying and addressing *vulnerabilities* swiftly. Additionally, *compliance* with our updated security policies, including mandatory *encryption* for sensitive communications, is essential for all departments.

To further protect our infrastructure, timely installation of security *patches* is now standard procedure. These patches are crucial in keeping our digital environment secure and resilient against evolving threats.

Your cooperation is vital in these efforts. Please be responsive to IT directives, clarify any queries with technical support, and remember to regularly update your device per instructions from our team.

Together, we can maintain a secure and safe digital workspace for everyone.

Best regards,

Craig Nakamoto
Cybersecurity Manager

PRO-TIP: Practice 'collocation hunting' in tech-related articles or reports. Look for common word pairings or phrases that frequently appear together. For example, collocations like 'digital threats', 'robust cybersecurity', and 'digital environment'. Understanding such collocations helps in catching the nuances of language used in the tech industry as well as using these terms more naturally in your conversations and writing.

ENGLISH AT THE SPEED OF TECH

UNIT 04 Cybersecurity Essentials

KEY VOCABULARY IN CONTEXT - PRACTICE

Complete the sentences below by filling in each blank with the best word from the choices provided. The first one is done for you.

1. . . . . client data to maintain *integrity* and prevent unauthorized access.

A. Diagnostic	B. Solution	C. Encrypt

2. Implementing a strong . . . . can promote better *integration* on our network.

A. debug	B. firewall	C. responsive

3. Handle . . . . documents with care, ensuring *compliance* with privacy laws.

A. clarify	B. solution	C. confidential

4. We must . . . . server activity to identify any potential *algorithm* threats.

A. responsive	B. monitor	C. assistance

5. Updating . . . . protection is essential for maintaining *firmware* integrity.

A. escalate	B. malware	C. precise

6. Analyze system . . . . to enhance our overall *diagnostic* capabilities.

A. debug	B. escalate	C. vulnerabilities

7. Ensure . . . . with data protection standards by conducting regular *updates*.

A. integrate	B. compliance	C. debug

8. Always . . . . customer information to uphold our ISMS *responsibilities*.

A. algorithm	B. beta	C. protect

9. Apply this security . . . . immediately to *debug* code and increase data integrity.

A. validate	B. patch	C. modularity

10. Ensure our database is . . . . by regularly updating encryption *algorithms*.

A. firmware	B. simulation	C. secure

Answer key p.59

ENGLISH AT THE SPEED OF TECH

UNIT 04 Cybersecurity Essentials

BUSINESS DIALOGUE

Read the dialogue and answer the comprehension questions that follow below.

Craig: Hello Julia, I wanted to discuss the new cybersecurity measures and training for your team. I sent an email brief about the updated firewall settings, did you get it okay?

Julia: Yes, Craig, no problem. The new initiatives sound pretty comprehensive. How exactly will this firewall protect our network?

Craig: It's designed to better protect against digital threats by using AI to monitor and block unauthorized access. The update ensures our confidential data remains secure.

Julia: Great, that's very reassuring. What about malware detection? How effective are the new systems at identifying vulnerabilities?

Craig: We've enhanced our malware detection capabilities as well. We can now more swiftly identify and address vulnerabilities, so user compliance with the new policies will be even more crucial.

Julia: Great! I've given everyone a heads up that some changes are coming. When will the team receive training on the new encryption protocols?

Craig: We're planning to arrange training sessions on encryption and the application of security patches by the end of this month. These measures will keep our digital environment secure and protect everyone from potential threats.

Julia: That sounds great, but will your department be able to help if anyone needs assistance or has questions about the update process?

Craig: Absolutely. I've asked the team to be responsive regarding any queries. It's vital to clarify issues early to keep compliance standards high.

Julia: Thanks for the information, Craig. I'll make sure my team stays informed and follows the new security protocols closely.

Comprehension questions

Q1   What is the primary purpose of the firewall mentioned by Craig?

Q2   How have the company's malware detection capabilities been enhanced?

Q3   What training is planned for the team regarding new cybersecurity protocols?

Q4   What does Julia reassure Craig of by the end of the dialogue?

Answer key p.60

ENGLISH AT THE SPEED OF TECH

UNIT | 04 Cybersecurity Essentials

PHRASE BANK

The phrases below will help you communicate more effectively in cybersecurity roles within the tech sector. They cover cybersecurity-related situations, from assessing security risks to implementing protective measures. Use them to more effectively articulate cyber-security strategies, engage in discussions about digital threats, and contribute to robust cybersecurity protocols.

Assessing Security Risks
We need to assess the ... for ...
Let's evaluate our firewall's ...
I'd like us to analyze the ...
Conducting a compliance audit ...

Discussing Cybersecurity Strategies
We need to strategize on ...
I propose upgrading ...
Let's discuss enhancing ...
We should consider increasing ...

Implementing Security Measures
We plan to implement a ...
Our team will encrypt ... on ...
We are planning to introduce ... by ...
To ensure compliance, we will ...

Providing Cybersecurity Training
We are planning to conduct training on ...
A session on ... is planned for ...
We will be offering training on ...
... training will be mandatory for ...

Communicating with IT Support
Please work with IT to troubleshoot ...
Please request IT to verify ...
Submit a ticket for IT to install ...
We need IT to ensure compliance with ...

Resolving Security Issues
Implementing ... should resolve the ...
Applying the security patch will address ...
Upgrading the ... should address ...
Testing has shown that ... will fix ...

Reporting Security Incidents
I'll prepare a report on the recent ...
It's critical to file a compliance report on ...
Please submit an incident report about ...
Be sure to document the ...

Addressing Concerns
Let's clarify ... concerns about the ...
I will address the questions regarding ...
We need to discuss concerns about ...
It's important to clarify ...

Cybersecurity Enhancements
We have scheduled the ... upgrade for ...
The ... enhancement will go live on ...
IT will install the .... update on ...
... guidelines will be revised by ...

Recommendations and Advice
We recommend ... to enhance security.
Cybersecurity experts suggest ...
It's crucial to ... for compliance reasons.
For optimal protection, we advise ...

CULTURE TIP

"In highly technical areas like cybersecurity, clear and precise communication is essential. By simplifying complex topics, you ensure that stakeholders fully understand the necessary security protocols. Opting for clear and direct language fosters effective communication, enhances understanding, and supports compliance. This approach empowers your organization to proactively address emerging cybersecurity challenges."

ENGLISH AT THE SPEED OF TECH

UNIT | 04 Cybersecurity Essentials

GRAMMAR FOCUS: FUTURE SIMPLE

The future simple tense is pivotal for discussing anticipated actions, planned updates, and potential threats. It's often used to convey plans or predictions about security measures. This tense is essential for articulating proactive strategies and responses to emerging cyber threats. In this context, the future simple is a tool for emphasizing forward-looking security practices in the dynamic world of cybersecurity.

1. We **will monitor** network traffic to promptly detect any unusual activities.

2. The team **will encrypt** data before transferring it to the cloud starting next week.

3. To enhance security, we **will implement** a new firewall by the end of Q1.

4. I **will update** the team's antivirus software regularly to protect against malware threats.

5. Our IT department **will deploy** a patch to address a recent software vulnerability.

> *Tip: The 'Will-When-What' Rule for Future Simple*
> *Will for Decision:* Use the future simple with *will* for decisions made at the moment of speaking.
> For example: "We will review the security protocols today."
> *When for Time:* Use the future simple to indicate *when* an action will happen.
> For example: "The system upgrade will happen next Tuesday."
> *What for Action:* Use the future simple to describe *what* action will be taken.
> For example: "Our team will resolve the network issue."

Unit 4 Task 5

GRAMMAR PRACTICE

Using the *Will/Decision-When/Time-What/Action* rule for future simple tense, determine which aspect applies to each sentence below and underline the relevant part(s). The first one is done for you.

1. **(What/Action)** Our team <u>will resolve the network issue by updating</u> the firmware.

2. (. . . . .) We've identified a new risk, so IT will update encryption standards today.

3. (. . . . .) An updated security patch will be deployed after the testing phase.

4. (. . . . .) Based on the compliance report we will revise security policies today.

5. (. . . . .) To reduce risks, we will monitor all system updates closely.

6. (. . . . .) Given this new vulnerability, we will deploy an updated patch today.

7. (. . . . .) The new protocol will be activated after the system reboots.

8. (. . . . .) Based on the threat report, we will upgrade malware settings today.

9. (. . . . .) The network security upgrade will take place tonight.

10. (. . . . .) We will enhance data protection by securing all critical files.

Answer key p.60

ENGLISH AT THE SPEED OF TECH

UNIT | 04 Cybersecurity Essentials

GRAMMAR IN ACTION: INCIDENT REPORT

Your team has detected signs of a pending Distributed Denial of Service (DoS) attack aimed at primary service platforms. Prepare an incident report outlining the steps you plan to take to avert the attack and protect the company's network.

Your report should include:

- *Threat Description: Briefly characterize the DoS attack, emphasizing its potential to disrupt client services.*
- *Initial Assessment: Describe initial plans, such as assessing network vulnerabilities and traffic patterns.*
- *Mitigation Plans: Detail your response, including measures like enhancing network defenses and rerouting.*
- *Expected Outcome: State the anticipated restoration of stable and secure service operations.*
- *Preventative Measures: Include long-term strategies such as upgrading network infrastructure and regular stress tests.*

Incident Report: Mitigating DDoS Threat ....

Threat Description: ....

....

Initial Assessment: ....

....

Mitigation Plans: ....

....

Expected Outcomes: ....

....

Preventative Measures: ....

....

Answer key p.60

54

ENGLISH AT THE SPEED OF TECH

EXPANSION ACTIVITY: ROLE-PLAY/SIMULATION

In this role-play, you'll simulate a meeting between the Cybersecurity Manager and a Department Head about implementing new cybersecurity protocols. The conversation will revolve around understanding and discussing the various aspects of the cybersecurity enhancements, including encryption, firewall upgrades, and the importance of compliance. Use the prompts provided to guide your dialogue, and focus on using the future simple tense to discuss upcoming plans and actions. Refer back to the Phrase Bank from this lesson to effectively communicate your role. This activity aims to develop a practical understanding of implementing cybersecurity measures and addressing concerns within an organizational setting. A model dialogue is also included for reference.

TEACHER NOTES: Expansion activities can be more effective when done with a partner, allowing you to practice the language and skills learned in this lesson more fully. If you don't have a teacher, consider practicing with a colleague or friend. Online teachers and tutors are also available at very reasonable rates these days. If you would like teacher notes to support your learning journey, just send an email to ***prospeak.author@outlook.com****, and we'll be happy to send you a PDF containing additional task notes, example responses, and expansion activity guidelines.*

ENGLISH AT THE SPEED OF TECH

UNIT | 04 Cybersecurity Essentials

Role A
Role: **Cybersecurity Manager**

Cybersecurity Protocol Implementation

Background

You are a Cybersecurity Manager tasked with implementing new cybersecurity protocols across your company. This initiative comes in response to a recent rise in digital threats. Your role involves explaining the importance of these protocols to the department heads, addressing any concerns, and ensuring a smooth implementation of the required protocols.

Prompts

Outline New Protocols: Start the meeting by discussing the need to encrypt all confidential information due to recent security breaches.

Discuss Firewall Upgrades: Explain how upgrading the firewall will protect against complex malware attacks and keep the company's network secure.

Elaborate on Continuous Monitoring: Share details about the new system that continuously monitors for vulnerabilities and potential security threats.

Emphasize Compliance Requirements: Stress that compliance with these new protocols is crucial for maintaining security standards.

Plan for Future Training: Inform the department heads about upcoming training sessions that will cover the practical aspects of these protocols.

NOTES

ENGLISH AT THE SPEED OF TECH

UNIT 04 Cybersecurity Essentials

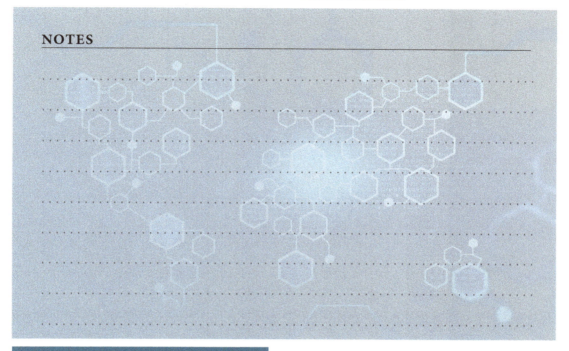

Role B	Role: **Department Head**

Cybersecurity Protocol Implementation

Background

As a Department Head, you are responsible for ensuring your team adapts to the new cybersecurity protocols. You need clarity on how these changes will impact your team's workflow and what support will be available during the transition. Use the prompts below to provide the Cybersecurity Manager with relevant information and ask for the same so you have what you need to explain to your team.

Prompts

Inquire about Data Encryption: Ask for specifics on how encrypting confidential information will affect access and if it will impact workflow efficiency.

Clarify Firewall Upgrade Details: Seek more information on the firewall upgrade, particularly how it might affect network speed or accessibility.

Express Monitoring Concerns: Discuss apprehensions about continuous monitoring, particularly privacy and integration with current operations.

Understand Compliance Steps: Question the exact steps your department needs to undertake to align with these new protocols.

Request Support and Training Details: Inquire about the available IT support during this transition and the specifics of the upcoming training sessions.

ENGLISH AT THE SPEED OF TECH

UNIT | 04 Cybersecurity Essentials

ROLE-PLAY/SIMULATION - SAMPLE DIALOGUE

Akio: Good morning, Sean. We're here to discuss how to implement the new encryption protocols in response to ongoing security concerns.

Sean: *Hi, Akio. I fully understand the need for security, but can you clarify how encrypting sensitive information will affect our work-flow?*

Akio: The process shouldn't impact your work-flow as it's designed to secure data in the background. Additionally, we are upgrading our firewall to more effectively handle malware threats.

Sean: *That sounds important. Will the upgrade impact network speed or accessibility?*

Akio: We've tested the upgrade and there won't be any impact on network performance. It will also provide continuous monitoring to identify vulnerabilities quickly.

Sean: *That's a clear benefit, but what privacy measures will be put in place with regard to continuous monitoring?*

Akio: Our compliance team will make sure that monitoring respects privacy norms while keeping our systems safe. These new protocols are crucial to maintaining our security standards.

Sean: *I agree, but what specific steps will my team need to take to comply?*

Akio: We are planning to conduct training on specific security practices to help everyone adapt smoothly.

Sean: *That's good to know. Will you be providing details on the IT support that will be available during the transition?*

Akio: Yes. IT support will be available to assist with any technical challenges. I'll also forward you a copy of our new training manual that includes an overview of the training we have planned.

Sean: *Excellent. That makes me more confident about this transition. I'll relay the information to my team and ask them to prepare for the upcoming training.*

Expansion - Design a Cybersecurity Awareness Campaign

The campaign should aim to improve employee understanding of cybersecurity practices like identifying malware and adhering to compliance standards. Use key vocabulary from this Unit along with other relevant technical terms to outline creative approaches such as informative posters on cybersecurity basics, interactive workshops, and newsletters updating staff on the latest cybersecurity threats and preventive measures. Practice delivering this proposal aloud, aiming for a 3-minute presentation that communicates your ideas clearly to a non-technical audience. This activity can be undertaken individually or with a partner/teacher for feedback. It will enable you to effectively utilize the language skills learned, helping you to convey the significance of cybersecurity in a professional and engaging manner. Good luck!

UNIT 04 Answer Key

KEY VOCABULARY IN CONTEXT

1) Encrypt client data to maintain *integrity* and prevent unauthorized access.

Incorrect: a) diagnostic is an adjective, not a verb as is needed here.

Incorrect: b) solution is a noun, not a verb.

2) Implementing a strong firewall can promote better *integration* on our network.

Incorrect: a) debug is a verb, not a noun as is needed here.

Incorrect: c) responsive is an adjective, not a noun.

3) Handle confidential documents with care, ensuring *compliance* with privacy laws.

Incorrect: a) clarify is a verb, not an adjective as is needed here.

Incorrect: b) solution is a noun, not an adjective.

4) We must monitor server activity to identify any potential *algorithm* threats.

Incorrect: a) responsive is an adjective, not a verb as is needed here.

Incorrect: c) assistance is a noun, not a verb.

5) Updating malware protection is essential for maintaining *firmware* integrity.

Incorrect: a) escalate is a verb, not a noun as is needed here.

Incorrect: c) precise is an adjective, not a noun.

6) Analyze system vulnerabilities to enhance our overall *diagnostic* capabilities.

Incorrect: a) debug is a verb, not a noun as is needed here.

Incorrect: b) escalate is a verb, not a noun.

7) Ensure compliance with data protection standards by conducting regular *updates*.

Incorrect: a) integrate is a verb, not a noun as is needed here.

Incorrect: c) debug is a verb, not a noun.

8) Always protect customer information to uphold our ISMS *responsibilities*.

Incorrect: a) algorithm is a noun, not a verb as is needed here.

Incorrect: b) beta (version) is an adjective, not a verb.

9) Apply this security patch immediately to *debug* code and increase data integrity.

Incorrect: a) validate is a verb, not a noun as is needed here.

Incorrect: c) modularity is a noun, but does not fit this context.

10) Ensure our database is secure by regularly updating encryption *algorithms*.

Incorrect: a) firmware is a noun, not an adjective as is needed here.

Incorrect: b) simulation is a noun, not an adjective.

NOTE: words in sentences 1-10 in ***italics*** are spaced repetition key words from previous units.

ENGLISH AT THE SPEED OF TECH

Unit 4 Task 4
BUSINESS DIALOGUE COMPREHENSION

Q1: What is the primary purpose of the firewall mentioned by Craig?
• *To protect the network with AI against digital threats and block unauthorized access.*
Rationale: Craig mentions the updated firewall uses AI to defend against digital threats.

Q2: How have the company's malware detection capabilities been enhanced?
• *It has improved its ability to swiftly identify and address vulnerabilities.*
Rationale: Craig explains that the enhancement in malware detection.

Q3: What training is planned for the team regarding new cybersecurity protocols?
• *Training sessions on encryption and the use of security patches.*
Rationale: Craig mentions arranging training sessions by the end of the month.

Q4: What does Julia reassure Craig of by the end of the dialogue?
• *That she will update her team and that they will follow the new security protocols closely.*
Rationale: Julia expresses commitment to her team adhering to the updated protocols.

Unit 4 Task 5
GRAMMAR PRACTICE

1) *(What/Action):* Our team will resolve the network issue by updating the firmware.

2) *(Will/Decision):* We've identified a new risk, so IT will update encryption standards today.

3) *(When/Time):* An updated security patch will be deployed after the testing phase.

4) *(Will/Decision):* Based on compliance reports we will revise security policies today.

5) *(What/Action):* To reduce risks, we will monitor all system updates closely.

6) *(Will/Decision):* Given this new vulnerability, we will deploy an updated patch today.

7) *(When/Time):* The new protocol will be activated after the system reboots.

8) *(Will/Decision):* Based on the threat report, we will upgrade malware settings today.

9) *(When/Time):* The network security upgrade will take place tonight.

10) *(What/Action):* We will enhance data protection by securing all client files.

Unit 4 Task 6
GRAMMAR IN ACTION: INCIDENT REPORT

Example model answer:
Incident Report: Anticipated Distributed Denial of Service (DoS) Attack

Threat Description: We have identified indications of an anticipated DoS attack that could disrupt client services and cause significant operational downtime.

Initial Assessment: We assessed a high probability of an attack. Several external IP addresses have been flagged as potential sources of this anticipated attack.

Mitigation Plans: We will implement additional firewalls to block malicious traffic. We will reroute traffic and coordinate with our Internet Service Provider (ISP) to trace and block incoming threats at their source.

Expected Outcome: We expect to maintain network integrity and will do our best to ensure uninterrupted client services.

Preventative Measures: We will enhance our cybersecurity infrastructure and conduct periodic network stress tests. We will initiate cybersecurity best practices training for all employees and establish ongoing network surveillance to detect and counteract potential threats.

Conclusion: Our cybersecurity team is fully prepared to tackle this anticipated threat. We are dedicated to safeguarding our digital assets and will do our best to ensure continuous service delivery to our clients.

Unit 04 Notes

....
....
....
....
....
....
....
....

Key takeaways

....
....
....
....

Useful Vocabulary

Use the text boxes below to write the word or phrase on the left and how it was used on the right.

Key words	Example sentence

Useful phrases	Example sentence

ENGLISH AT THE SPEED OF TECH

UNIT | 05 The Startup Pitch

LEARNING OBJECTIVES

Welcome to Unit 5: The Startup Pitch.
This lesson explores the dynamic language of business startups, highlighting useful expressions and the present perfect tense to bridge past experiences with present achievements. You'll navigate the art of crafting compelling 'elevator-pitch' presentations and business proposals, sharpening your ability to articulate innovative ideas succinctly. This unit is designed to enhance your presentation skills, helping you to engage and persuade in the fast-paced world of startups. Doing so is a key competence for succeeding in the ever-evolving domain of Big Tech.

WARM-UP

Before diving into "The Startup Pitch," take a moment to think about the questions below. Your responses will provide context for our journey into the world of startup pitches and business proposals. Note down your responses so you can refer back to them later:

- What unique challenges do you think startups face when presenting their ideas to potential investors?
- Consider the last startup pitch that impressed you. What aspects of their presentation or business idea stood out?

DID YOU KNOW...

"... the concept of the 'elevator pitch' originated in Hollywood, where screenwriters would hang out in hotel lobbies to pitch movie ideas to studio executives during brief elevator rides? This concept has since evolved into a crucial business skill. Typically spanning 30 seconds to two minutes, an elevator pitch emphasizes the art of concise, persuasive communication and has gained immense popularity in the business world. Mastering this skill can make the difference between capturing or missing out on key opportunities."

ENGLISH AT THE SPEED OF TECH

UNIT | 05 The Startup Pitch

KEY VOCABULARY IN CONTEXT

capital (n), equity (n), compelling (adj), persuasive (adj), monetize (v), traction (n), persuade (v), scalability (n), startup (n), pitch (v)

Read this email to see the words used in a start-up pitch context.

Subject: Startup with Exceptional Growth Potential

Dear [Investor's Name],

I am reaching out with an exclusive opportunity to look at a *startup* that is rapidly gaining *traction* in the [industry sector]. NexGenTech offers *compelling* innovation and a *persuasive* strategy that is ready to disrupt the market.

The NexGenTech startup possesses remarkable *scalability* that is supported by a data-driven, strategic vision for *monetization*. We are eager to discuss how an *equity* share in our venture promises significant returns for early investors.

I would be more than happy to arrange a meeting with our team to *pitch* our vision, showcase our business model, and answers any questions you may have. Rest assured, our startup is *compliant* with industry standards, *secure*, and positioned to make a lasting impact.

Would you be available for a presentation in the near future? I am confident that our vision and potential for tangible success will resonate with your interests.

Your time and consideration are greatly appreciated.

Best regards,

Taylor Morgan
Chief Visionary Officer

PRO-TIP: *Begin integrating the words and phrases you find useful into your emails, meetings, and presentations. Such 'real-world application' is not just about learning new words; it's about embedding them in your daily professional communications. Actively using these terms in contexts that matter to you ensures better retention and a deeper understanding. By doing so, you're proactively building them into your business English vocabulary. This approach is vital for achieving fluency and confidence in business settings, especially in the dynamic world of big tech where clear and compelling communication is key.*

ENGLISH AT THE SPEED OF TECH

UNIT | 05 The Startup Pitch

KEY VOCABULARY IN CONTEXT - PRACTICE

Complete the sentences below by filling in each blank with the best word from the choices provided. The first one is done for you.

1. Our . . . . has *streamlined* its operations to better meet market demands.

A. clarified	B. iterating	**C. startup**

2. We have . . . . potential partners by *clarifying* our unique value proposition.

A. agile	B. persuaded	C. compliance

3. The . . . . design of our product has *validated* its market fit.

A. encryption	B. compelling	C. monitor

4. Our . . . . to investors has *secured* substantial funding for expansion.

A. debug	B. firmware	C. pitch

5. Gaining . . . . online, we've *monitored* user feedback to improve features.

A. responsive	B. traction	C. algorithm

6. We have . . . . our services by offering *precise* and tailored solutions.

A. diagnostic	B. integrate	C. monetized

7. The . . . . of our software has been enhanced by *iterating* on user feedback.

A. scalability	B. encrypt	C. validate

8. Acquiring . . . . investment has been pivotal in *debugging* our app.

A. monitor	B. patch	C. equity

9. Our team has . . . . communicated the *innovative* aspects of our product.

A. persuasively	B. solution	C. clarify

10. Raising . . . . was easier after integrating *analytics* into our business model.

A. firewall	B. capital	C. escalate

Answer key p.73

ENGLISH AT THE SPEED OF TECH

UNIT 05 The Startup Pitch

BUSINESS DIALOGUE

Read the dialogue and answer the comprehension questions that follow below.

Taylor: Thank you, that concludes my presentation. I hope it showcased NexGenTech's potential and I'm happy to take any questions.

Investor: Thank you, Taylor. The presentation was quite compelling. Could you detail how much market traction you've gained?

Taylor: Certainly. We've secured terms with TechCorp and InnovateX and leveraged social media, resulting in a 25% rise in brand engagement.

Investor: Sounds good. On capital, what is your funding goal, and how do you plan to utilize it?

Taylor: We're aiming for $12 million in capital to expand our operations, mainly focusing on team growth and product enhancement.

Investor: And regarding equity, what percentage are you offering for this investment?

Taylor: We propose an initial 15% equity stake that offers a good balance between our current value and future potential.

Investor: How have you monetized your product to date, and what about future revenue plans?

Taylor: We've generated $1.5 million via new subscriptions and future plans include exploring partnerships to increase reach by 30% while adding new products.

Investor: Thank you, Taylor. Your presentation was insightful, and your company shows a lot of potential. I'll review the details with our partners and get back to you with our decision soon.

Taylor: We're excited about the possibility of collaborating with you and look forward to your decision. Thank you again for your time.

Comprehension questions

Q1 What strategies did NexGenTech use to gain market traction?

Q2 What is the funding goal of NexGenTech, and for what purpose?

Q3 What percentage of equity is NexGenTech offering for the investment?

Q4 What are NexGenTech's future plans for revenue generation?

Answer key p.74

ENGLISH AT THE SPEED OF TECH

UNIT | 05 The Startup Pitch

PHRASE BANK

The phrases below will assist you in navigating the dynamic world of startup pitches and business proposals. They cover a range of situations, from introducing innovative start-up ideas to discussing investment opportunities. Use the phrases to pitch your startup's potential, discuss growth and scalability, and present compelling solutions. Whether you're seeking investment or planning your marketing strategy, these phrases will help convey your vision more persuasively.

Introducing a Startup Idea
Having identified a gap in the market, we ...
Our team has developed a unique ...
We created an innovative approach to ...
Our team has focused on solving ...

Highlighting Scalability
Our design has allowed us to scale by ...
We have ensured scalability through ...
We can support expanded users by. ..
Scalability has been a key focus ...

Presenting to Investors
In our pitch today, we will highlight ...
Our presentation will showcase ...
We plan to demonstrate our impact on ...
Anticipating investor concerns, we have ...

Talking about Terms
For your investment, we are offering ...
In exchange for capital, we propose ...
The equity stake will provide ...
Potential returns on an investment are ...

Managing Data Security
We have made security a top priority by ...
We have implemented robust ...
All assets have solid protection against ...
To safeguard user data, we regularly ...

Discussing Market Traction
We've gained significant traction by ...
Our users have expanded rapidly due to ...
Since launch, we've seen growing ...
Feedback has been very positive, with ...

Monetization Strategies
We have monetized our services by ...
Our strategy has proven effective by ...
Through strategic partnerships, we have ...
The subscription model has yielded ...

Clarifying Product Features
Let me explain how our technology ...
The unique features of our product are ...
To explain further, our solution offers ...
Our software stands out due to its ...

Addressing Risks
We have identified and mitigated risks by ...
We offer sustainability through ...
In terms of risk management, we ...
To address possible concerns, we have ...

Seeking Feedback and Support
We welcome feedback on how to ...
Your insights on ... would be very valuable.
We look forward to any suggestions on ...
Based on user feedback, we have ...

CULTURE TIP

"In your startup pitch, address key points from your audience's perspective. Focus on benefits over features, emphasizing scalability and monetization potential. Use compelling language to illustrate how investing capital or equity in your startup promises growth and success. Craft your pitch as an irresistible narrative of opportunity."

ENGLISH AT THE SPEED OF TECH

UNIT | 05 The Startup Pitch

GRAMMAR FOCUS: PRESENT PERFECT

The present perfect tense verb is key for linking past actions to current outcomes. It's often used to express completed action or achievements that impact the present. The present perfect is essential for showing how past efforts contribute to current business standing and strategies. In the fast-paced startup environment, the present perfect helps to illustrate how previous experiences and milestones are shaping ongoing growth and future prospects.

1. Our startup **has attracted** significant capital since its launch last year.

2. Our company **has gained** considerable traction in the market over the past months.

3. Since pitching our idea, we **have persuaded** several key investors to join us.

> *Tip: The 'Experience-Progress-Result' Rule for Present Perfect*
> *Experience for History:* Use the present perfect to talk about experiences or achievements that have relevance to the present.
> For example: "Our startup has attracted significant venture capital."
> *Progress for Ongoing Development:* Use it to show progress or ongoing actions that started in the past and continue to the present.
> For example: "We have been developing this technology for two years."
> *Result for Current State:* Use it to emphasize the present result of past actions.
> For example: "We have secured three patents for our product."

Unit 5 Task 5

GRAMMAR PRACTICE

Using the *Experience-Progress-Result* rule for present perfect, look at the sentences below and decide which one of the three apply and then underline the relevant part(s) of the sentence. The first one is done for you.

1. (Experience) We have raised significant capital, reflecting our innovative strategy.

2. (. . . . . .) Our company has established strong equity, a result of agile strategies.

3. (. . . . . .) We have developed a compelling business plan, gaining investor interest.

4. (. . . . . .) Our new protocol has become highly successful, securing several patents.

5. (. . . . . .) We have been monetizing our software license due to its scalability.

6. (. . . . . .) Our market traction has been growing, reflecting ongoing innovation.

7. (. . . . . .) The team has persuaded numerous clients with our product's functionality.

8. (. . . . . .) The scalability of our solution has led to increased market share.

9. (. . . . . .) We have been pitching our idea, consistently iterating as we go.

10. (. . . . . .) Since our launch, we have raised capital from various investors.

Answer key p.74

ENGLISH AT THE SPEED OF TECH

UNIT | 05 The Startup Pitch

GRAMMAR IN ACTION: BUSINESS PLAN UPDATE

Using the present perfect tense, update the business plan below to reflect your company's current status and achievements.

For example, use your own ideas to update sections like **Company Overview** to reflect the expansion of the business, **Product and Services** to include any new features or products added, and **Market Analysis** to discuss how the market has evolved, etc. Focus on achievements, growth, and any significant changes since the original plan was made.

Write your update and then check it against the model answer on page 74. The **Company Overview** is done for you:

Business Plan Summary: TechWave Solutions.

Company Overview: TechWave Solutions was established in 2018 as a technology startup focusing on developing innovative software solutions for small to medium-sized businesses.

Company Overview: TechWave Solutions, established in 2018, has grown significantly as a technology startup. We have expanded our focus to include innovative software solutions not only for small to medium-sized businesses but also for larger enterprises.

Product and Services

Our main product, "BizFlow," was designed to streamline business operations. BizFlow offers features like inventory management, customer relationship management (CRM), and data analytics.

Market Analysis

When we began, our market research indicated a significant demand for affordable and user-friendly business management software among small businesses.

Marketing Strategy

Our initial marketing strategy focused on digital marketing campaigns and partnerships with local business organizations to reach our target audience.

Financial Projections

The financial projections for the first three years forecasted steady growth in sales and customer base, with a break-even point expected in the second year.

Milestones

Key milestones included the launch of BizFlow, securing our first 100 customers, and our first round of investor funding.

Answer key p.74

ENGLISH AT THE SPEED OF TECH

UNIT | 05 The Startup Pitch

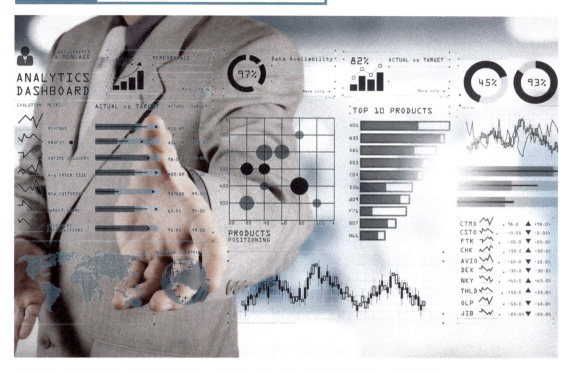

EXPANSION ACTIVITY: ROLE-PLAY/SIMULATION

In this role-play, you'll simulate a pitch meeting between a startup Partner, Alex Turner, and an Angel Investor, Mia Chen. The meeting conversation will center around presenting and evaluating a new software solution designed to streamline business work-flows. Use the provided prompts to guide your dialogue, focusing on using the present perfect tense to discuss achievements and developments. Refer back to the Phrase Bank from this lesson to effectively articulate your startup's potential and address the investor's queries. This activity aims to develop a practical understanding of pitching innovative ideas and offering investment opportunities in a startup environment. A model dialogue is also included for reference.

TEACHER NOTES: *Expansion activities can be more effective when done with a partner, allowing you to practice the language and skills learned in this lesson more fully. If you don't have a teacher, consider practicing with a colleague or friend. Online teachers and tutors are also available at very reasonable rates these days. If you would like teacher notes to support your learning journey, just send an email to **prospeak.author@outlook.com**, and we'll be happy to send you a PDF containing additional task notes, example responses, and expansion activity guidelines.*

ENGLISH AT THE SPEED OF TECH

UNIT | 05 The Startup Pitch

Role A   Role: **Startup Partner - Alex Turner**

Startup Investor Pitch

Background

As a Partner in an emerging tech startup specializing in innovative software solutions designed to streamline business work flows, you've successfully navigated the early stages of product development and market entry. You've secured initial funding and developed a robust prototype that has attracted attention in the tech industry. Now, you're seeking a significant investment to fuel growth and market expansion. This meeting with the investor is a pivotal moment to secure funding that could launch your startup into its next phase of development.

Prompts

Start Your Pitch: Thank Mia for her time. Talk about the core idea and technology behind your unique software solution, TaskStream.

Market Traction: Explain how your startup has begun to gain traction in the market and share some feedback from early users.

Monetization and Scalability: Elaborate on your tiered subscription model, strategic partnerships, and potential for scalability.

Investor Advantages: Highlight the advantages for investors, including potential returns and equity shares.

Risk Management: Respond to any questions about data security, risk management, and the startup's long-term prospects.

NOTES

ENGLISH AT THE SPEED OF TECH

UNIT | 05 The Startup Pitch

NOTES
_____

| Role B | Role: Investor - Mia Chen |

Startup Investor Pitch

Background

As an Angel investor, you've built a reputation for identifying promising tech ventures. You're particularly interested in startups that offer innovative solutions to common business challenges. This tech startup has caught your attention with their cutting-edge software solution. You've been impressed with their progress and initial market success. You're meeting to look deeper into the startup's market viability, growth potential, financial forecasts, and to understand how investing in this startup could benefit your portfolio.

Prompts

Startup Distinction: Ask what sets their software solution apart in the crowded tech market.

Market Feedback: Inquire about the startup's current market traction and user feedback.

Financial Model: Seek details on the revenue model, scalability of the product, and long-term profitability.

Equity Clarification: Clarify what kind of equity share you would receive in exchange for your investment.

Risk and Sustainability: Voice any concerns regarding the startup's sustainability and risk factors, including data security.

ENGLISH AT THE SPEED OF TECH

UNIT | 05 The Startup Pitch

ROLE-PLAY/SIMULATION - SAMPLE DIALOGUE

Alex: Thank you for your interest in our startup, Mia. Having identified a gap in the market, we have developed a unique software solution called TaskStream that optimizes business work-flows.

Mia: *It sounds intriguing, Alex. What sets TaskStream apart in the competitive productivity software market?*

Alex: We've created an innovative AI-driven approach that streamlines task management and enhances team collaboration. Our user base has expanded by 30% due to its intuitive design and AI-based task prioritization.

Mia: *Interesting! Can you share how you've monetized TaskStream so far?*

Alex: Certainly. We use a tiered subscription model, from $15 to $50 per user per month, and have strategic partnerships with HubSpot and Asana that have helped us integrate into existing business ecosystems.

Mia: *Those are impressive partnerships. In terms of investment, what equity are you offering?*

Alex: Our terms include a 12% equity share. The capital will be used to boost our marketing efforts and software development, including advanced analytics and customizable work-flows.

Mia: *I See. How about data security, Alex? With the rise in malware threats, that's a key concern for any business software?*

Alex: Absolutely, Mia. Security is a top priority. We use 256-bit encryption and conduct quarterly security audits by third-party experts to ensure compliance with the latest standards.

Mia: *Your pitch is persuasive and the product seems compelling, Alex. I'll review the proposal with my team and get back to you soon.*

Alex: Thank you, Mia. We believe TaskStream has the potential to revolutionize productivity in the workplace and look forward to the opportunity of working with you.

Expansion - Create a Startup Business Proposal

Craft your own business proposal for a tech startup idea. Focus on a unique product or service, applying key vocabulary from this chapter and the present perfect tense to highlight your startup's development and future plans. Your proposal should include an innovative concept, a clear business model that includes monetization strategies, and a unique selling proposition that sets your idea apart. Discuss scalability, capital and equity options, and marketing strategies to gain sales traction. Conclude with a persuasive summary emphasizing the investment appeal of your startup. Practice presenting your proposal aloud for about 3 minutes, aiming for clarity and engagement. This can be done individually or with a partner/teacher for feedback, enhancing your ability to communicate effectively in the startup environment. Good luck!

ENGLISH AT THE SPEED OF TECH

KEY VOCABULARY IN CONTEXT

1) Our startup has *streamlined* **its operations to better meet market demands.**

Incorrect: a) clarified is a verb, not a noun as is needed here.

Incorrect: b) iterating is a verb, not a noun.

2) We have persuaded potential partners by *clarifying* **our unique value proposition.**

Incorrect: a) agile is used as an adjective in the context of 'methodology'.

Incorrect: c) compliance is a noun, not a verb.

3) The compelling design of our product has *validated* **its market fit.**

Incorrect: a) encryption is a noun, not an adjective as is needed here.

Incorrect: c) monitor is a verb, not an adjective.

4) Our pitch to investors has *secured* **substantial funding for expansion.**

Incorrect: a) debug is a verb, not a noun as is needed here.

Incorrect: b) firmware is a noun, but does not fit this context.

5) Gaining traction online, we've *monitored* **user feedback to improve features.**

Incorrect: a) responsive is an adjective, not a noun as is needed here.

Incorrect: c) algorithm is a noun, but does not fit this context.

6) We have monetized our services by *offering* **precise and tailored solutions.**

Incorrect: a) diagnostic is an adjective, not a verb as is needed here.

Incorrect: b) integrate is a verb, but is the wrong tense to fit here.

7) The scalability of our software has been *enhanced* **by iterating on user feedback.**

Incorrect: b) encrypt is a verb, not an adjective as is needed here.

Incorrect: c) validate is a verb, not an adjective.

8) Acquiring equity investment has been pivotal in *debugging* **our app.**

Incorrect: a) monitor is a verb, not a noun as is needed here.

Incorrect: b) patch is a noun but does not fit as a compound of 'investment'.

9) Our team has persuasively communicated the *innovative* **aspects of our product.**

Incorrect: b) solution is a noun, not an adverb as is needed here.

Incorrect: c) clarify is a verb, not an adverb.

10) Raising capital was easier after integrating *analytics* **into our business model.**

Incorrect: a) firewall is a noun, but does not fit this context.

Incorrect: c) escalate is a verb, not a noun as is needed here.

NOTE: words in sentences 1-10 in *italics* are spaced repetition key words from previous units.

ENGLISH AT THE SPEED OF TECH

UNIT 05 Answer Key

Unit 5 Task 4

BUSINESS DIALOGUE COMPREHENSION

Q1: What strategies did NexGenTech use to gain market traction?

• *They secured terms with TechCorp and InnovateX and leveraged social media.*
Rationale: Taylor mentions these strategies specifically.

Q2: What is the funding goal of NexGenTech, and for what purpose?
• *$12 million, for expanding operations, team growth, and product enhancement.*
Rationale: Taylor states this goal and its purpose.

Q3: What percentage of equity is NexGenTech offering for the investment?
• *NexGenTech is offering a 15% equity stake.*
Rationale: Taylor mentions this proposed equity stake.

Q4: What are NexGenTech's future plans for revenue generation?

• *Exploring partnerships to increase reach by 30% while adding new products.*
Rationale: Taylor outlines these future plans when asked by the investor.

Unit 5 Task 5

GRAMMAR PRACTICE

1. (**Experience**) We have raised significant capital, reflecting our innovative strategy.

2. (**Result**) Our company has established strong equity, a result of agile strategies.

3. (**Experience**) We have developed a compelling business plan, gaining investor interest.

4. (**Result**) Our new protocol has become very persuasive, securing several patents.

5. (**Progress**) We have been monetizing our software license, enhancing its scalability.

6. (**Progress**) Our market traction has been growing, reflecting ongoing innovation.

7. (**Experience**) Our team has persuaded numerous clients with our product's functionality.

8. (**Result**) The scalability of our solution has led to increased market share.

9. (**Progress**) We have been pitching our idea, constantly iterating as we go.

10. (**Experience**) Since our launch, we have raised capital from various investors.

Unit 5 Task 6

GRAMMAR IN ACTION: BUSINESS PLAN UPDATE

Example model answer:

Business Plan Summary: TechWave Solutions

Product and Services: Since our inception, we have continually enhanced "BizFlow," our flagship product, adding advanced features such as AI-driven analytics and cloud integration. Additionally, we have launched two new products, "CustomerConnect" and "InventoryPro," further diversifying our service offerings.

Market Analysis: Our market research has consistently shown an increasing demand for our software solutions, especially in emerging markets. We have adapted our approach to target these new segments effectively.

Marketing Strategy: Our marketing efforts have evolved over time. We have established strong online presence and partnerships with major industry players, leading to increased brand recognition.

Financial Projections: We have surpassed our initial financial projections, achieving a 30% annual growth rate. Our customer base has expanded beyond 500 enterprises, and we reached our break-even point within the first 18 months.

Milestones: Key milestones we have achieved include the successful launch of BizFlow's cloud-based version, securing over 500 global customers, and completing a second round of funding with prominent investors. Additionally, we have won two industry awards for innovation in software development.

Unit 05 Notes

....
....
....
....
....
....
....
....

Key takeaways

....
....
....
....

Useful Vocabulary

Use the text boxes below to write the word or phrase on the left and how it was used on the right.

Key words	Example sentence

Useful phrases	Example sentence

ENGLISH AT THE SPEED OF TECH
UNIT | 06 At the Tech Conference

LEARNING OBJECTIVES

Welcome to Unit 6: At the Tech Conference. This unit goes deeper into the language and communication of tech events, focusing on essential phrases and grammar for discussing planned activities. You will learn how to more effectively engage with peers at a tech conference and practice email communications in this context. Building on earlier units, this lesson prepares you for more successful networking and collaboration in the fast-paced and exciting world of technology conferences and other networking events.

WARM-UP

Before exploring "At the Tech Conference," consider the following questions to guide your learning in this chapter. Reflecting on these questions will help frame your understanding of navigating tech conferences effectively. Make a note of your thoughts, as they will be useful to refer back to:

- How do you typically approach people when networking at tech conferences? What do you say to strike up a conversation?
- How do you manage follow-ups after meeting professionals at tech conferences?

DID YOU KNOW...

"... that Singapore, Vienna, and Barcelona are setting remarkable records in the world of tech conferences? Singapore has impressively maintained its status as the top city for conventions globally for nine years in a row! Vienna, not just the city of music and culture, hosts more than 2,000 large-scale tech meetings and events each year. Meanwhile, Barcelona, Spain's second-largest city, is rapidly rising in the tech-conference world and ambitiously aims to become the leading conference center in the tech industry."

ENGLISH AT THE SPEED OF TECH

UNIT 06 At the Tech Conference

KEY VOCABULARY IN CONTEXT

panel (n), workshop (n), **keynote (n)**, network (v), sponsor (n), breakout (adj), exhibit (v/n), session (n), delegate (n), informative (adj)

Read this announcement to see the key words used in a conference context.

Announcement: 202x Tech Conference - "Innovate and Network"

Dear *Delegate*,

We are thrilled to invite you to the "Innovate and *Network*" Tech Conference, an event that showcases the latest in technology and innovation. Scheduled for November, and made possible thanks to our generous *sponsors*, the event will feature an array of leading-edge *sessions* and *workshops* led by industry experts.

During the conference, our *keynote* speakers will be discussing how start-ups can monetize their innovative ideas and secure capital investment. *Breakout* sessions will focus on recent advancements in encryption, firewall security, and malware protection. Additionally, we are excited to host a *panel* on the scalability of new technologies in our fast-evolving digital landscape.

Networking opportunities will also be highlighted, allowing a broad range of tech firms and innovators to exchange ideas and solutions. Our main *exhibit* area will showcase disruptive technologies and provide insights into the latest product developments.

Looking to the future, this conference will be an invaluable platform for participants to engage, learn, and network. We are certain it will be an *informative* and unforgettable experience for everyone involved.

Best regards,

James Lee
Conference Organizer

PRO-TIP: End study units with a 'vocabulary reflection.' Write a brief essay or journal entry about a current trend in Big Tech, using as many new words from the textbook as possible. Reflecting on your learning journey helps cement these words in your memory and showcases your progress in mastering business English vocabulary relevant to your field.

ENGLISH AT THE SPEED OF TECH

UNIT 06 At the Tech Conference

KEY VOCABULARY IN CONTEXT - PRACTICE

Complete the sentences below by filling in each blank with the best word from the choices provided. The first one is done for you.

1. Next month, we will be hosting a . . . . that *clarifies* emerging tech trends.

A. encrypt	**B. panel**	C. scalable

2. We will be holding a . . . . on *streamlining* our processes.

A. workshop	B. firewall	C. algorithm

3. Our CEO will be delivering the . . . . on *disruptive* technologies.

A. diagnostic	B. keynote	C. prototype

4. I will be . . . . with peers and vendors to *benchmark* our progress.

A. networking	B. solution	C. firmware

5. A tech firm will be . . . . the event and showcasing their *scalable* solutions.

A. iterate	B. analytics	C. sponsoring

6. In the PM . . . . session, we will be discussing software *modularity*.

A. innovate	B. breakout	C. monitor

7. We will be . . . . our latest *prototype* at the tech fair next week.

A. agile	B. disrupting	C. exhibiting

8. The . . . . on cybersecurity will be discussing *firewall* technology.

A. innovate	B. patch	C. session

9. . . . . will be exploring *encryption* methods in our special seminar.

A. Scalable	B. Benchmarks	C. Delegates

10. Our session will be providing . . . . insights into algorithm development.

A. modularity	B. informative	C. encrypt

Answer key p.87

ENGLISH AT THE SPEED OF TECH

UNIT 06 At the Tech Conference

BUSINESS DIALOGUE

Read the dialogue and answer the comprehension questions that follow below.

James: Good morning, Francis. I'm James Lee. We're looking forward to your keynote on disruptive technologies.

Francis: Hi James, it's great to be involved. My keynote will explore how startups can persuasively pitch their innovations to investors.

James: That's a vital topic for our audience. We also have you scheduled for a panel on the scalability of emerging digital technologies.

Francis: Yes, I'm excited about that. Additionally, I'll be leading a workshop focused on integrating agile planning in product development.

James: I'm looking forward to it. Our delegates, especially those in startups, are eager to network and learn from experienced professionals like yourself.

Francis: Networking is always a highlight for me. By the way, are there any sessions on cybersecurity planned?

James: Yes, indeed, there's a breakout session covering the latest in firewall and encryption technologies.

Francis: Excellent. As a conference sponsor, my company is thrilled to exhibit our latest prototype which aligns with emerging security trends.

James: We appreciate your company's support. The exhibit area is a perfect place for showcasing such leading-edge technology.

Francis: I'm also looking forward to the other presentations. It's very positive to see other companies innovating with interesting solutions.

James: Absolutely, it's the diversity of ideas and solutions that makes this conference so valuable. We're all about fostering innovation and collaboration.

Comprehension questions

Q1	What topic will Francis be discussing in the keynote presentation?
Q2	What is the theme of the workshop that will be led by Francis?
Q3	Which technology topics will be covered in the breakout session?
Q4	What will Francis' company be showcasing at the conference?

Answer key p.88

ENGLISH AT THE SPEED OF TECH

UNIT | 06 At the Tech Conference

PHRASE BANK

The phrases below should help improve your communication skills at conferences. They cover situations from starting conversations to presenting your company's innovations. Use them to confidently navigate discussions about technology trends, engage with potential partners, or discuss your ideas and opinions. Whether you're exploring new solutions or representing your company, these phrases will help to convey your message with improved impact and precision.

Initial Greetings
Nice to meet you, I'm ...
Hello, I'm ... from ...
It's a pleasure to meet you.
I'm excited to be here at ...

Introducing Yourself
My name's ..., I work in ...
I'm ... from ..., specializing in ...
I focus on ... at ...
I lead the ... team at ...

Discussing Interests, Expertise
My main interest lies in ...
I've been working on ... recently
I specialize in ... technology
My recent projects involve ...

Sharing Insights, Opinions
I believe that ... will ...
My experience with ... has shown that ...
In my opinion, ... is crucial for ...
From what I've seen, ... is trending ...

Asking Others for Perspectives
What's your take on ...?
Have you worked with. .. before?
How do you approach ...?
What are your thoughts on ...?

Discussing Future Plans
We will be launching ... soon
Our team is focusing on ... next quarter
I'll be working on ... in the coming months
We're planning to expand into ...

Exploring Opportunities
There could be synergy between us in ...
Have you considered partnering on ...?
We're looking for collaboration in ...
Your expertise in ... would complement ...

Exchanging Contact Information
Can I get your LinkedIn contact so ...?
Here's my card, let's discuss ... further
I'd love to stay in touch about ...
Would you be interested in a follow-up on ...

Planning a Follow-up
Let's set up a meeting to discuss ...
I'll send you more information on ...
I'll follow up with you next week about ...
Let's schedule a call to continue our ...

Concluding the Conversation
Thanks for the great conversation about ...
I enjoyed discussing ... with you.
Look forward to continuing our chat on ...
It was insightful to learn about ...

CULTURE TIP

"Networking well at tech or other conferences means more than just making small talk; it's about connecting with your peers. Aim to share your ideas clearly and concisely, but also make the time to listen intently. It's this kind of vibrant exchange with people from around the world that can turn conferences into a chance for personal and professional growth while building on your network and circle of influence"

ENGLISH AT THE SPEED OF TECH

UNIT | 06 At the Tech Conference

GRAMMAR FOCUS: FUTURE CONTINUOUS

The future continuous tense is essential for discussing ongoing activities in a future context. It's often used to talk about actions that will be happening at a particular time in the future. For example, "Next quarter, we will be implementing a new software update." This tense is perfect for conveying plans and actions that are expected to take place, reflecting a forward-looking perspective. The future continuous helps paint a picture of anticipated progress and continuous development.

1. Next week, we **will be focusing** on AI advancements in our panel discussion.

2. Our tech team **will be conducting** a cybersecurity workshop on Thursday morning.

3. At the next monthly meeting, our team **will be presenting** the latest cloud solutions.

> ### Tip: The 'Planned, Ongoing, and Concurrent' Rule for Future Continuous
>
> *Planned Actions:* Use 'will be' + '-ing' form for scheduled or planned activities.
> Example: "Next month, we will be launching our new software."
>
> *Ongoing Events:* Apply it for actions occurring at a specific future time.
> Example: "During the conference, we will be demonstrating our latest technology."
>
> *Concurrent Actions:* Use it to describe actions that will be ongoing and happening at the same time.
> Example: "I will be attending the seminar when the product launch begins."

Unit 6 Task 5

GRAMMAR PRACTICE

Using the *Planned-Ongoing-Concurrent* rule for future continuous, look at the sentences below and decide which one of the three apply and then underline the relevant part(s) of the sentence. The first one is done for you.

1. (Concurrent) During the breakout session, we will be checking user analytics.

2. (. . . . . .) Our team will be networking with vendors to secure new partnerships.

3. (. . . . . .) During today's session, developers will be working on the new update.

4. (. . . . . .) While we are at the workshop, our Dev team will be iterating new versions.

5. (. . . . . .) We will be exhibiting our scalable solution at next week's technology fair.

6. (. . . . . .) While our CEO delivers the keynote, we will be prototyping in the lab.

7. (. . . . . .) Our sponsor will be showcasing their compelling AI solution all day.

8. (. . . . . .) We will be discussing startup trends in tomorrow's breakout session.

9. (. . . . . .) While the panel discusses cloud tech, we will be updating our software.

10. (. . . . . .) Delegates will be presenting an informative update on market trends

Answer key p.88

ENGLISH AT THE SPEED OF TECH

UNIT 06 At the Tech Conference

GRAMMAR IN ACTION: PRESENTER QUESTIONS

Use the activity below to practice making questions for presenters at sessions you would like to attend at an upcoming conference. Look at the session topics below and choose those in the morning and afternoon that you would like to attend.

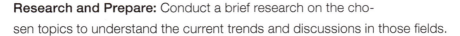

TechVision 202x: Pioneering the Future

AM Sessions

The Blockchain Beyond Crypto - Diverse Applications
Internet of Things (IoT): Smart Cities and Beyond
Cloud Computing: Trends and Innovations for 202x

PM Sessions

Cybersecurity in the Age of AI: Staying Ahead
Big Data Analytics: Transforming Business Intelligence
Wearable Tech: The Future of Personal Computing

Research and Prepare: Conduct a brief research on the chosen topics to understand the current trends and discussions in those fields.

Develop Your Questions: Write-up some questions for each session you plan to attend. Use the future continuous tense where appropriate. For example:
"In the Internet of Things session, In what ways will IoT be changing urban living in smart cities?"
"In the Big Data session, what strategies will you be discussing to handle data privacy concerns?"

Tailor Your Point of View: Ensure your questions are insightful, open-ended, and reflect your professional interests or curiosities. Check your answers with more examples on p.88

Practice and Feedback: Practice and share your questions for discussion and feedback.

....

....

....

....

....

....

....

Answer key p.88

ENGLISH AT THE SPEED OF TECH

UNIT | 06 At the Tech Conference

EXPANSION ACTIVITY: ROLE-PLAY/SIMULATION

In this role-play, you'll simulate a networking interaction during a break at the "Tech-Vision 202x: Pioneering the Future" conference. The conversation will revolve around sharing insights from the sessions, exploring common interests in technology trends, and discussing potential business collaborations. Use the provided prompts to guide your dialogue, incorporating the future continuous tense to discuss plans and expectations. Refer back to the Phrase Bank from this lesson to effectively communicate your professional insights and engage in discussions about future collaborations. This activity is designed to enhance your networking skills in a tech conference environment. A model dialogue is also included for reference.

*TEACHER NOTES: Expansion activities can be more effective when done with a partner, allowing you to practice the language and skills learned in this lesson more fully. If you don't have a teacher, consider practicing with a colleague or friend. Online teachers and tutors are also available at very reasonable rates these days. If you would like teacher notes to support your learning journey, just send an email to **prospeak.author@outlook.com**, and we'll be happy to send you a PDF containing additional task notes, example responses, and expansion activity guidelines.*

ENGLISH AT THE SPEED OF TECH

UNIT | 06 At the Tech Conference

Role A	Role: **Teri - Cloud Computing Expert**

Networking at 'TechVision' Conference

Background

As an experienced cloud computing expert with CloudNet Solutions, you are keenly interested in the latest trends and innovations in cloud technology. At CloudNet, you were the lead on several projects related to cloud infrastructure and services, making them more efficient and scalable. You've just left the "Cloud Computing: Trends and Innovations" session. Eager to network, you're looking to share session insights and explore opportunities for business collaboration. During the break between sessions you strike up a conversation with another conference delegate.

Prompts

Introduce yourself: Mention your role at CloudNet Solutions and the session you have just come out of.

Session insights: Share takeaways from the cloud computing session and ask what Liam is working on at his company.

Collaboration exploration: Explore common interests in cloud technologies and potential collaboration areas.

Contact exchange: Suggest exchanging business cards for future discussions and partnerships.

NOTES

....

....

....

....

....

....

....

....

ENGLISH AT THE SPEED OF TECH

UNIT 06 At the Tech Conference

Role B	Role: **Liam - Big Data Specialist**

Networking at 'TechVision' Conference

Background
Working at DataStream Analytics as a Big Data Specialist, you have a strong interest in how big data is transforming industries and integrating with other technologies like IoT and cloud computing. You've played a crucial role in developing advanced analytics solutions that harness the power of big data for predictive insights and decision-making. Attending the "TechVision" conference, you're particularly focused on sessions about Big Data and IoT. Meeting a cloud computing expert during a break presents a perfect opportunity to discuss how cloud computing can complement big data strategies and the challenges involved in integrating these technologies.

Prompts
Respond to introduction: Share your role at DataStream Analytics and your expertise in Big Data and IoT.

Insight sharing: Offer your insights on integrating cloud computing with Big Data solutions.

Collaboration interest: Express interest in the potential benefits of a collaboration between your companies.

Contact exchange: Agree to exchange contacts and propose a meeting to explore joint projects.

ENGLISH AT THE SPEED OF TECH

UNIT 06 At the Tech Conference

ROLE-PLAY/SIMULATION - SAMPLE DIALOGUE

Teri: Hello, I'm Teri from CloudNet Solutions. I've just come out of the session on cloud trends. What's your area of interest?

Liam: *Hi Sean, I'm Liam from DataStream Analytics. My focus is on big-data, especially its integration with IoT. How was the session on cloud computing? I missed that one.*

Teri: Very interesting. It was focused on scalability given the exponential growth of Internet data these days. What areas are you currently working on at DataStream?

Liam: *Well, we're focused on encryption methods to secure our IoT devices in the cloud, as well as exploring how AI can help to manage our technologies. Does CloudNet intersect with any of these areas?*

Teri: Absolutely. We're actually hosting a workshop on cloud-based solutions for big data management next month. It'll be very informative, especially for companies like yours, if you might be interested?

Liam: *Hmm, that does sound interesting. Shall we exchange contact information and schedule a follow-up call?*

Teri: Great idea. Here's my LinkedIn. Let's set up a time to discuss further.

Liam: *Actually, I'll be attending the keynote on disruptive technologies from 4pm. Maybe we can catch up after that for a quick chat?*

Teri: Sounds perfect. I'll be in the CloudNet exhibit booth showcasing our latest project on cloud security. Let's meet there.

Liam: *Nice! Looking forward to it, Teri.*

Teri: Great! See you at the exhibit area, Liam.

Expansion - Conference Follow-Up Email

Write a follow-up email to a 'contact you met' during one of the sessions at the TechVision 202x conference from Task 6. Your email should:

• *Begin with a personalized greeting, mentioning the session where you met.*
• *Briefly recap a point or topic from the session that sparked your mutual interest.*
• *Mention a specific discussion or idea you shared during your conversation.*
• *Propose a follow-up action, such as a meeting, collaboration, or further discussion on a shared topic of interest.*
• *Conclude with a professional closing and an invitation for a response.*

Focus on making your email friendly, engaging, and relevant to the session's topic and your shared professional interests. This task can be performed individually or with a partner/teacher for feedback, aiming to improve your ability to nurture and expand your professional network in the tech industry. Good luck!

KEY VOCABULARY IN CONTEXT

Q1: Next month, we will be hosting a panel that *clarifies* emerging tech trends.

Incorrect: a) encrypt is a verb, not a noun as is needed here.

Incorrect: c) scalable is an adjective, not a noun.

Q2: We will be holding a workshop on *streamlining* our processes.

Incorrect: b) firewall is a noun, but does not fit this context.

Incorrect: c) algorithm is a noun, but does not fit this context.

Q3: Our CEO will be holding the keynote on *disruptive* technologies.

Incorrect: a) diagnostic is typically an adjective, not a noun as is needed here.

Incorrect: c) prototype is a noun, but does not fit this context.

Q4: I will be networking with peers and vendors to *benchmark* our progress.

Incorrect: b) solution is a noun, not a verb as is needed here.

Incorrect: c) firmware is a noun, not a verb.

Q5: A tech firm will be sponsoring the event and showcasing their *scalable* solutions.

Incorrect: a) iterate is a verb, but the wrong tense, and does not fit this context.

Incorrect: b) analytics is a noun, not a verb as is needed here.

Q6: In the PM breakout session, we will be discussing software and design *modularity*.

Incorrect: a) innovate is a verb, not an adjective as is needed here.

Incorrect: c) monitor is a verb, not an adjective.

Q7: We will be exhibiting our latest *prototype* at the tech fair next week.

Incorrect: a) agile (method) is an adjective, not a verb as is needed here.

Incorrect: b) disrupting is a verb, but does not fit this context.

Q8: The session on cybersecurity will be discussing *firewall* technology.

Incorrect: a) innovate is a verb, not a noun as is needed here.

Incorrect: b) patch is a noun, but does not fit this context.

Q9: Delegates will be exploring *encryption* methods in our special seminar.

Incorrect: a) scalable is an adjective, not a noun as is needed here.

Incorrect: b) benchmarks is a noun, but does not fit this context.

Q10: Our session will be providing informative insights into *algorithm* development.

Incorrect: a) modularity is a noun, not an adjective as is needed here.

Incorrect: c) encrypt is a verb, not an adjective.

NOTE: words in sentences 1-10 in *italics* are spaced repetition key words from previous units.

ENGLISH AT THE SPEED OF TECH

UNIT 06 Answer Key

BUSINESS DIALOGUE COMPREHENSION

Q1: What topic will Francis be discussing in his keynote presentation?
• *How startups can persuasively pitch their innovations to investors.*
Rationale: Francis states this in the dialogue.

Q2: What is the theme of the workshop led by Francis?
• *Integrating agile planning in product development.*
Rationale: Francis says, "I'll be leading a workshop focused on..."

Q3: Which technology topics will be covered in the breakout session?
• *The latest in firewall and encryption technologies.*
Rationale: James confirms this after being asked by Francis.

Q4: What will Francis' company be showcasing at the conference?
• *Their latest prototype (which aligns with emerging security trends).*
Rationale: Francis says, "my company is thrilled to exhibit our latest prototype".

GRAMMAR PRACTICE

1. (**Concurrent**) During the breakout session, we will be checking user analytics.

2. (**Planned**) Our team will be networking with vendors to secure new partnerships.

3. (**Ongoing**) During today's session, developers will be debugging the new software update.

4. (**Concurrent**) While we are at the workshop, our Dev team will be iterating new versions.

5. (**Planned**) We will be exhibiting our scalable solution at next week's technology fair.

6. (**Concurrent**) While our CEO delivers the keynote, we will be prototyping in the lab.

7. (**Ongoing**) Our sponsor will be showcasing their compelling AI solution all day.

8. (**Planned**) We will be discussing startup trends in tomorrow's breakout session.

9. (**Concurrent**) While the panel discusses cloud tech, we will be updating our firewall.

10. (**Ongoing**) Delegates will be presenting an informative update on market trends.

GRAMMAR IN ACTION: PRESENTER QUESTIONS

Sample questions
• How will the blockchain be transforming industries outside finance in the next five years?
• What new blockchain applications will be covered in this session?
• How will IoT be integrating with everyday life for enhanced experiences?
• What challenges in deploying IoT in smart cities will be discussed?
• What emerging cloud computing trends will be highlighted?
• How will cloud computing evolve for big data and AI?
• How will AI be utilized in future cybersecurity strategies?
• What AI-related cybersecurity threats will be the focus?
• How will big data analytics reshape future business decision-making?
• What new big data analytics tools and technologies will be discussed?
• How will wearable tech integrate into daily life for productivity?
• What advancements in wearable tech will be the session's focus?

Unit 06 Notes

....

....

....

....

....

....

....

....

Key takeaways

....

....

....

....

Useful Vocabulary

Use the text boxes below to write the word or phrase on the left and how it was used on the right.

Key words	Example sentence

Useful phrases	Example sentence

ENGLISH AT THE SPEED OF TECH

UNIT | 07 Product Launch and Marketing

LEARNING OBJECTIVES

Welcome to Unit 7: Product Launch and Marketing. This lesson delves into the language of tech product introductions and marketing strategies. It introduces key words and phrases useful for discussions around product launches and campaigns, focusing on the past continuous tense to effectively set the scene in marketing narratives. This unit is designed to develop and refine your professional communication skills, essential for creating persuasive product launch stories and crafting impactful marketing materials that elevate your product's success.

Unit 7 Task 1

WARM-UP

Before starting the unit on "Product Launch and Marketing," consider these questions to set the context for our lesson. Reflecting on them will lay the groundwork for the language and skills we will cover about product launches and marketing strategies in the tech industry. Note down your thoughts, as they will be useful to look back on as we go:

- What key elements do you consider crucial for a successful tech product launch?

- How do you think marketing strategies differ for tech products compared to other industries?

DID YOU KNOW...

"... that Pokémon Go, launched in July 2016, achieved an impressive $207 million in its first month and amassed over 500 million downloads by the end of its first year? The popular game now boasts a global user base exceeding one billion. Niantic, the developer of Pokémon Go, was originally an internal startup within Google before becoming independent in 2015. Known for its augmented reality (AR) and location-based games, Niantic's continuous updates and special events helped Pokémon Go surpass $4 billion in revenue by 2020, significantly influencing social behavior and physical activity among its vast user base."

ENGLISH AT THE SPEED OF TECH

UNIT 07 Product Launch and Marketing

KEY VOCABULARY IN CONTEXT

branding (n), launch (v), campaign (n), engagement (n), metrics (n), conversion (n), strategic (adj), targeting (v), promotion (n), viral (adj)

Read this memo to see the key words used in a Product Launch context.

Memo: Upcoming Social Media Product Launch Strategy

Hi Emily,

As we were planning the *launch* of our new tech product, I wanted to share the marketing strategy we've been developing for our social media *campaign*. Our approach focuses on maximizing *engagement* and *conversion* through *strategic targeting* and compelling content.

We're planning a series of *viral promotions* across various platforms, each tailored to the unique *branding* of our product. As of last week, the campaign was being fine-tuned, with the objective to create a buzz well before the official launch. We're targeting tech-savvy consumers and potential influencers from related tech fields.

Key *metrics* will be closely monitored to track the campaign's traction and scalability. We've included a mix of informative and entertaining content to ensure high engagement levels. The initial feedback from our beta testers was encouraging, as they found the product innovative and the campaign persuasive.

We're also scheduling a series of interactive discussion panels as part of our digital outreach to provide deeper insights into the product. This aligns with our goal to educate and persuade our audience about the unique features of our product.

Looking forward to discussing this further and iterating on our ideas.

Best regards,

Jordan Lee

PRO-TIP: *Start a vocabulary-centered discussion group with your peers in the tech sector. Each week, select a relevant tech topic and delve into it using the new vocabulary you've been learning. Encourage members to bring along real-world examples or recent tech developments to discuss. This method of 'collaborative learning' not only deepens your own understanding of technical terms but also gives you a practical platform to practice and apply these terms in meaningful, professional discussions.*

ENGLISH AT THE SPEED OF TECH

UNIT 07 Product Launch and Marketing

KEY VOCABULARY IN CONTEXT - PRACTICE

Complete the sentences below by filling in each blank with the best word from the choices provided. The first one is done for you.

1. . . . . was being discussed to focus on the product's *innovative* solutions.

| **A. Branding** | B. Network | C. Escalate |

2. We were . . . . new initiatives, with significant *equity* investment.

| A. firmware | B. launching | C. compliance |

3. The marketing . . . . was being *monitored* for high engagement.

| A. campaign | B. session | C. delegate |

4. Customer . . . . was *escalating* during the product launch phase.

| A. prototype | B. engagement | C. benchmark |

5. . . . . were being *analyzed* to track the campaign's effectiveness.

| A. Patent | B. Iterate | C. Metrics |

6. Our . . . . rate was improving because we *targeted* key demographics.

| A. conversion | B. escalate | C. encrypt |

7. A . . . . plan was being formulated for our *viral* promotion.

| A. innovate | B. strategic | C. iterate |

8. To target the right *audience*, we were preparing . . . . content.

| A. persuasive | B. iterate | C. revise |

9. An exclusive . . . . was being *prototyped* for early adopters.

| A. escalate | B. monitor | C. promotion |

10. Aiming for a . . . . impact, we were leveraging social media *influencers*.

| A. viral | B. debug | C. encrypt |

Answer key p.101

ENGLISH AT THE SPEED OF TECH

UNIT 07 Product Launch and Marketing

BUSINESS DIALOGUE

Read the dialogue and answer the comprehension questions that follow below.

Jordan: Hi Emily, we were just finalizing our social media campaign plan. The branding strategy is really shaping up.

Emily: That's great to hear, Jordan. How are the metrics looking for engagement rates?

Jordan: They're improving. We were looking to target more tech-savvy consumers, and it's showing in our conversion rates.

Emily: Excellent. And the promotion we were planning for early adopters, is it ready?

Jordan: Yes, we've been working on the viral strategy we discussed and are scheduling some panel discussions for deeper insights.

Emily: I like that approach. It's very strategic. Are we also considering scalability factors for moving to larger audiences?

Jordan: Absolutely. We were discussing that with our sponsor. They're excited about the launch event.

Emily: Perfect. Let's keep iterating on these ideas and stay responsive to the market feedback our analysts are collecting.

Jordan: Agreed. Don't forget we'll also be exhibiting at the tech fair next month to showcase our latest project.

Emily: I'm looking forward to seeing it. Let's keep this momentum going!

Jordan: Definitely. We'll regroup after the fair for further planning and updates.

Emily: Great! By the way, can you send over the updated analytics report, please.

Jordan: Certainly, Emily. I'll compile the latest data and email it to you this afternoon.

Emily: Thanks, Jordan!

Comprehension questions

Q1   What was the main focus of Jordan and Emily's discussion?

Q2   What does Jordan mention as showing improvement?

Q3   What promotion approach is being aimed at early adopters?

Q4   What request does Emily make at the end of the conversation?

Answer key p.102

ENGLISH AT THE SPEED OF TECH

UNIT | 07 Product Launch and Marketing

PHRASE BANK

The phrases below should help improve your communication skills at conferences. They cover situations from starting conversations to presenting your company's innovations. Use them to confidently navigate discussions about technology trends, engage with potential partners, or discuss your ideas and opinions. Whether you're exploring new solutions or representing your company, these phrases will help to convey your message with improved impact and precision.

Giving an Update
We were finalizing ...
Last week, we focused on ...
Our team has been working on ...
I wanted to share ...

Evaluating Marketing Efforts
We're seeing improvements in ...
Our conversion rates were ...
We were targeting ...
The campaign's traction is ...

Addressing Challenges
We faced several challenges ...
We implemented adaptive strategies to ...
The team was quick to address ...
We tackled ... issues by ...

Reporting Metrics and Analysis
Through key metrics analysis, we ...
Our metrics indicate ...
Our analysis clearly shows ...
We have been closely monitoring ...

Discussing Campaign Impact
Our viral strategy achieved ...
We are expecting .... from ...
By innovating with ... we ...
Through viral marketing we ...

Discussing Branding Strategies
We've been refining ...
Our branding strategy involves ...
The digital team was engaging ...
We're adopting new ...

Planning Promotions
Our promotional efforts included ...
We've been working on a ...
To attract early adopters, we ...
Through strategic promotions we ...

Exploring Future Plans
In the next ..., we will be ...
We're looking forward to ...
We're discussing ... with ...
Our future plans involve ...

Highlighting Engagement
By maximizing engagement we ...
Our engagement numbers show ...
Through improved conversion we ...
By enhancing audience engagement ...

Reviewing Collaborative Efforts
The team effectively collaborated on ...
Our joint iterations on ... achieved ...
By cooperating with ... we were able to ...
Collaborating on ... resulted in ...

CULTURE TIP

"In the global tech marketplace, clear and impactful messaging is key during product launches and marketing. Focus on articulating the unique solutions your product offers. Tailoring your language with this in mind helps in conveying the benefits of your product, making it relevant and desirable across diverse markets. A well-articulated message that focuses on solutions enhances global market success, establishing your product in its respective niche."

ENGLISH AT THE SPEED OF TECH

UNIT | 07 Product Launch and Marketing

GRAMMAR FOCUS: PAST CONTINUOUS

The past continuous tense is often used to describe activities that were in progress at a specific time in the past, such as ongoing situations, discussions, or extended actions. By emphasizing ongoing past actions and their contexts, this tense effectively captures scenarios that were unfolding, providing a comprehensive understanding of the circumstances surrounding business operations and events, and adding depth and clarity to your narrative.

1. Our team **was analyzing** metrics to improve our marketing campaign's impact.

2. While reviewing the plans, we **were focusing** on targeting the right audience.

3. During the meeting, we **were outlining** the key steps for a successful launch.

> ### Tip: The 'While, When, and For' Rule for Past Continuous
>
> *While for Simultaneous Actions:* Use the past continuous with 'while' to describe actions happening at the same time.
> Example: "While I was coding, my colleague was testing."
> *When for Interruptions:* Use 'when' to introduce interruptions in ongoing past actions.
> Example: "I was writing a report when the phone rang."
> *For for Duration:* Use 'for' to indicate the length of time an action was ongoing.
> Example: "We were working on the project for several hours."

Unit 7 Task 5

GRAMMAR PRACTICE

Using the *While-When-For* rule for past continuous, look at the sentences below and decide which one of the three apply and then underline the relevant part(s) of the sentence. The first one is done for you.

1. (Duration) We were building engagement for months before the campaign started.

2. (. . . . . .) We were strategizing when the latest user analytics arrived.

3. (. . . . . .) While we were working on branding, marketing was planning the launch.

4. (. . . . . .) We were improving conversion methods for the entire month of June.

5. (. . . . . .) While we were finalizing the campaign, IT was analyzing metrics.

6. (. . . . . .) We were planning promotion ideas when key user feedback arrived.

7. (. . . . . .) We were planning the launch for several weeks over the summer.

8. (. . . . . .) While gathering metrics, we were refining our conversion approach.

9. (. . . . . .) While targeting key markets, the creative team worked on promotions.

10. (. . . . . .) We were going viral when the competitors introduced new discounts.

Answer key p.102

ENGLISH AT THE SPEED OF TECH

UNIT | 07 Product Launch and Marketing

GRAMMAR IN ACTION: UPDATE

Scenario: As a marketing team leader at a tech company, your task is to update your manager about the ongoing product launch.

Prepare the Update: Write a brief report on the team's activities in the past week, focusing on the past continuous tense to describe ongoing tasks.

Key Actions: Highlight actions related to branding, engagement, analyzing metrics, and developing strategic marketing plans.

Challenges and Solutions: Mention any challenges the team faced and the steps taken to address them.

Future Plans: Conclude with an overview of upcoming tasks, using future continuous tense for forward-looking statements.

Overall: ....

....

....

....

Key Actions: ....

....

....

....

Challenges and Solutions: ....

....

....

Future Plans: ....

....

....

Answer key p.102

ENGLISH AT THE SPEED OF TECH

UNIT | 07 Product Launch and Marketing

EXPANSION ACTIVITY: ROLE-PLAY/SIMULATION

In this role-play, you'll be simulating a product launch update meeting between Franz, a Marketing Manager, and Jinhan, a Marketing Team Leader. The conversation will focus on discussing the progress and challenges related to the ongoing product launch. Use the provided prompts to guide your dialogue, effectively using the past continuous tense to describe past actions and the future continuous tense for upcoming plans. This activity aims to develop your skills in strategic discussion, problem-solving, and future planning in the context of product launch and marketing. A model dialogue is also included for reference.

> *TEACHER NOTES: Expansion activities can be more effective when done with a partner, allowing you to practice the language and skills learned in this lesson more fully. If you don't have a teacher, consider practicing with a colleague or friend. Online teachers and tutors are also available at very reasonable rates these days. If you would like teacher notes to support your learning journey, just send an email to **prospeak.author@outlook.com**, and we'll be happy to send you a PDF containing additional task notes, example responses, and expansion activity guidelines.*

ENGLISH AT THE SPEED OF TECH

Role A

Role: **Franz - Marketing Manager**

Product Launch Update Meeting

Background

As the marketing manager overseeing the product launch, you're tasked with guiding your team's strategy, ensuring alignment with the product's strengths. You've noted areas needing improvement in branding, particularly regarding public engagement and metrics analysis. You aim to explore these areas in detail with Jinhan, understanding the challenges faced and the adaptive strategies implemented. You're keen to discuss plans for viral promotions and targeting specific consumer demographics.

Prompts

Evaluate Branding Evolution: Discuss the team's progress in evolving the product's branding, including refining the brand message and digital presence.

Review Engagement Strategies: Examine the team's strategies to enhance audience engagement, including the effectiveness of social media campaigns.

Discuss Viral Campaigns: Explore the development and expected impact of upcoming viral promotions, including innovative marketing techniques.

Tackle Challenges: Address challenges faced in engagement and branding, including adaptive strategies the team employed.

Strategize Future Moves: Talk about future marketing plans, including approaches to expand the campaign's reach and enhance customer targeting.

NOTES

ENGLISH AT THE SPEED OF TECH

UNIT 07 Product Launch and Marketing

NOTES

Role B	Role: **Jinhan, Marketing Team Leader**

Product Launch Update Meeting

Background
As the marketing team leader, you've been actively engaged in various aspects of the product launch, focusing on strategic branding and audience engagement. Your team faced challenges with fluctuating engagement metrics, prompting a shift in content strategy. You're prepared to discuss these challenges with Franz, outlining the solutions your team implemented and plans for increasing campaign scalability. You'll also be sharing insights into upcoming promotional activities and strategies for reaching a broader audience.

Prompts
Report on Branding Strategy: Share the recent changes in branding strategy, including the adoption of new digital marketing tools and user engagement techniques.

Explain Metrics Fluctuations: Provide insights into the fluctuations in engagement metrics, including how they were identified and addressed.

Highlight Promotional Plans: Discuss the specifics of the upcoming viral promotions, including innovative approaches and anticipated outcomes.

Detail Adaptive Strategies: Elaborate on how the team adapted to challenges, including specific problem-solving steps and any pivot in strategy.

Share Future Marketing Plans: Talk about the upcoming marketing initiatives, including the focus areas and expected impact on market presence.

ENGLISH AT THE SPEED OF TECH

UNIT | 07 Product Launch and Marketing

ROLE-PLAY/SIMULATION - SAMPLE DIALOGUE

Franz: Hi Jinhan, I hope you're well. We were discussing the team's branding strategy earlier. How's it coming along?

Jinhan: *Hello, Franz. The team was working on refining our digital presence and adopting new marketing tools.*

Franz: That's great to hear. We were also focusing on audience engagement. How effective have our social media campaigns been?

Jinhan: *We've seen some promising metrics. While enhancing our content strategy, we noticed a rise in user engagement.*

Franz: Excellent. And what about the viral promotions we were planning? Are they ready for launch?

Jinhan: *Yes, we were finalizing them last week. The campaign includes some innovative techniques to boost our online traction.*

Franz: Good to know. We've faced some challenges in branding, though. How did the team adapt?

Jinhan: *We were quick to implement adaptive strategies, focusing on targeted marketing and leveraging analytics insights.*

Franz: It sounds like we're on the right track. Let's keep iterating on these ideas and ensure scalability for a wider audience.

Jinhan: *Agreed. I'll share more details about our upcoming promotional activities and marketing initiatives in our next meeting.*

Franz: Looking forward to it, Jinhan. Let's ensure our campaign resonates well with our target demographics.

Jinhan: *Definitely. I'll compile a comprehensive report on our marketing plans and insights for our next discussion.*

Expansion - Tech Product Press Release

Write a press release for a new 'tech product' you're launching. Your press release should:

• Start with an engaging headline that sums up the product.

• Include an opening paragraph summarizing the product, its unique selling points, and the launch date.

• Highlight key features and benefits, using vocabulary and the past continuous tense from this chapter.

• Address the target audience, market needs, and how your product stands out.

• Conclude with a call to action, inviting readers to attend a launch event.

Focus on making your press release informative and engaging, reflecting the product's innovation and relevance. This task can be done individually or with a partner/teacher for feedback, enhancing your skills in creating effective marketing materials. Good luck!

KEY VOCABULARY IN CONTEXT

Q1: Branding was being discussed to focus on the product's *innovative* solutions

Incorrect: b) network is a noun, but does not fit this context.

Incorrect: c) escalate is a verb, not a noun as is needed here.

Q2: We were launching our new prototypes, with significant *equity* investment.

Incorrect: a) firmware is a noun, not a verb as is needed here.

Incorrect: c) compliance is a noun, not a verb.

Q3: The marketing campaign was being *monitored* for high engagement.

Incorrect: b) session is a noun, but not the best choice for this context.

Incorrect: c) delegate is a noun, but does not fit this context.

Q4: Customer engagement was *escalating* during the product launch phase.

Incorrect: a) prototype is a noun, but does not fit this context.

Incorrect: c) benchmark is a noun but does not fit this context.

Q5: Metrics were being *analyzed* to track the campaign's effectiveness.

Incorrect: a) patent is a noun, but does not fit this context and is singular.

Incorrect: b) iterate is a verb, not a noun as is needed here.

Q6: Our conversion rate was improving as we were *targeting* key demographics.

Incorrect: b) escalate is a verb, not part of a noun phrase as is needed here.

Incorrect: c) encrypt is a verb, not a noun.

Q7: A strategic plan was being formulated for our *viral* promotion.

Incorrect: a) innovate is a verb, not an adjective as is needed here.

Incorrect: c) iterate is a verb, not an adjective.

Q8: To target the right *audience*, we were preparing persuasive content.

Incorrect: b) iterate is a verb, not an adjective as is needed here.

Incorrect: c) revise is a verb, not an adjective.

Q9: An exclusive promotion was being *prototyped* for early adopters.

Incorrect: a) escalate is a verb, not a noun as is needed here.

Incorrect: b) monitor is verb, not a noun.

Q10: Aiming for a viral impact, we were leveraging social media *influencers*.

Incorrect: b) debug is a verb, not an adjective as is needed here.

Incorrect: c) encrypt is a verb, not an adjective.

NOTE: words in sentences 1-10 in *italics* are spaced repetition key words from previous units.

ENGLISH AT THE SPEED OF TECH

UNIT 07 Answer Key

BUSINESS DIALOGUE COMPREHENSION

Q1: What was the main focus of Jordan and Emily's discussion?
• *Finalizing their social media campaign plan and branding strategy.*
Rationale: Jordan starts the conversation by mentioning these two areas.

Q2: What does Jordan mention as showing improvement?
• *Engagement rates and conversion rates.*
Rationale: Jordan notes improvements in both.

Q3: What promotion approach is being aimed at early adopters?
• *A viral strategy along with scheduling panel discussions.*
Rationale: Jordan confirms the viral strategy and mentions organizing panel discussions.

Q4: What request does Emily make at the end of the conversation?
• *She asks Jordan to send over the updated analytics report.*
Rationale: Emily concludes the conversation by requesting the report from Jordan.

GRAMMAR PRACTICE

1. (**Duration**) We were building engagement for months before the campaign start.

2. (**Interruption**) We were strategizing when the latest user analytics arrived.

3. (**Simultaneous**) While we were working on branding, marketing was planning the launch.

4. (**Duration**) We were improving conversion methods for the entire month of June.

5. (**Simultaneous**) While we were finalizing the campaign, IT was analyzing metrics.

6. (**Interruption**) We were planning promotion ideas when key user feedback arrived.

7. (**Duration**) We were planning the launch for several weeks over the summer.

8. (**Simultaneous**) While gathering metrics, we were refining our conversion approach.

9. (**Simultaneous**) While targeting key markets, the creative team worked on promotions.

10. (**Interruption**) We were going viral when the competitors introduced new discounts.

GRAMMAR IN ACTION: MARKETING UPDATE

Example model answer:

Hi Marco,

I hope this finds you well. Here's an update on our marketing team's progress over the past week:

Branding and Engagement: Last week, *we were working hard* to enhance our branding approach, ensuring it aligns more effectively with our product identity. Concurrently, the digital team *was actively engaging* audiences on social media platforms.

Metrics Analysis: *We were closely monitoring* engagement metrics, tweaking our content strategy to optimize impact. The strategic marketing plan is nearing completion, and *we will soon begin targeting* our key consumer segments.

Challenges and Solutions: Faced with fluctuating metrics, we were quick to implement adaptive strategies, showing promising improvements.

Looking Forward: In the coming week, *we will be finalizing* the overall marketing plan and kick-starting the promotional activities for our product launch.

Best,

Sara
Marketing Team Leader

Unit 07 Notes

....
....
....
....
....
....
....
....

Key takeaways

....
....
....
....

Useful Vocabulary

Use the text boxes below to write the word or phrase on the left and how it was used on the right.

Key words	Example sentence

Useful phrases	Example sentence

ENGLISH AT THE SPEED OF TECH

UNIT | 08 AI and Robotics

LEARNING OBJECTIVES

Welcome to Unit 8: AI and Robotics. This unit explores the evolving language of this transformative technology, introducing key terminology and concepts. You'll practice the present perfect continuous tense, important for describing ongoing developments and trends in projects and technology. This unit also aims to sharpen your communication skills for complex AI concepts and discussing the continuous evolution in robotics. Use this lesson to engage with cutting-edge technology and enhance your professional discourse in the fast-paced world of AI and robotics.

WARM-UP

Before diving into Unit 8: AI and Robotics, consider the following questions.

Thinking about them now will help set the stage for our exploration into this fascinating field. Make a note of your ideas. Keeping a record of your initial responses will be a helpful reference that you can look back on as we progress through the unit:

- What recent advancements in AI have you found most impactful in your work?
- What role do you see robotics playing in the future of the tech industry?

DID YOU KNOW...

"... that OpenAI's ChatGPT achieved 1 million users in just five days, making it one of the fastest-growing consumer applications ever? Additionally, the website generated a remarkable 1.7 billion visits in October 2023. Nowadays, ChatGPT boasts over 100 million users and receives nearly 1.5 billion monthly visitors. More than 2 million developers are using OpenAI's tools to build their own AI products and businesses, and more than 92 percent of Fortune 500 companies are using OpenAI. ChatGPT averages savings of up to $70,000 annually for companies through automation and efficiency, showcasing its vast capabilities in transforming business operations."

ENGLISH AT THE SPEED OF TECH

UNIT 08 AI and Robotics

KEY VOCABULARY IN CONTEXT

logic (n), interact (v), neural (adj), robot (n), cognitive (adj), interface (n), intelligence (n), ethics (n), automate (v), AI (n)

Read this Tech Brief to see the key words used in an AI and Robotics context.

Subject: Current AI Developments and Robotics Integration

To: All Staff

Dear Team,

Our work in the *AI* and Robotics division has been making significant strides.

We have been focusing on integrating advanced *neural* networks into our *robot* designs, enhancing their *cognitive* capabilities. This work focuses on creating responsive AI *interfaces* that can *interact* more naturally with humans. Our latest project in AI *logic* has been showing promising results, particularly in efforts to *automate* complex decision-making processes and improve system *intelligence*.

Ethical considerations remain at the forefront, especially regarding AI and its applications. We've been collaborating with the *ethics* committee to ensure compliance with industry standards.

In recent months, we've seen substantial progress in AI logic application. We've been experimenting with scalable and secure solutions, including encryption protocols to protect our intellectual property.

Looking ahead, we're exploring strategic partnerships to expand our network and showcase our innovative technology in upcoming exhibitions. We're also developing strategies to secure our intellectual property.

The team has been working hard on these initiatives, and I look forward to updating you further in our next session.

Best regards,

Alex Kim, Director of AI and Robotics

PRO-TIP: Consider a task-based learning project with a focus on AI and Robotics, a proven method to reinforce language skills. Start a mini-project such as creating a simple AI chatbot or designing a robotic process automation system concept in English. Working with peers, apply newly learned vocabulary in context, reinforcing your understanding of terminology while enhancing your overall language proficiency.

ENGLISH AT THE SPEED OF TECH

UNIT 08 AI and Robotics

KEY VOCABULARY IN CONTEXT - PRACTICE

Complete the sentences below by filling in each blank with the best word from the choices provided. The first one is done for you.

1. We have been using disruptive . . . . to *interface* with AI and robots.

A. logic	B. escalate	C. iterate

2. Engineers have been trying to . . . . with AI using *responsive* parameters.

A. campaign	B. patent	C. interact

3. The team has been studying . . . . networks to enhance *encryption*.

A. metrics	B. neural	C. streamline

4. The . . . . has been navigating the research area without human *input*.

A. pitch	B. robot	C. escalate

5. Researchers have been exploring . . . . AI to improve *campaign* strategies.

A. clarify	B. monetize	C. cognitive

6. We have been using code and logic as an . . . . to robotic *solutions*.

A. interface	B. escalate	C. innovate

7. Our team has been using artificial . . . . to enhance *predictive* analytics.

A. monetize	B. escalate	C. intelligence

8. We have been discussing . . . . in AI to align with our business *strategy*.

A. ethics	B. launch	C. debug

9. Our QA team has been working to . . . . processes that *validate* data sets.

A. solution	B. confidential	C. automate

10. The design team has been using . . . . to *iterate* prototyping procedures.

A. persuade	B. AI	C. strategic

Answer key p.115

ENGLISH AT THE SPEED OF TECH

UNIT 08 AI and Robotics

BUSINESS DIALOGUE

Read the dialogue and answer the comprehension questions that follow below.

Alex: Good morning, Ken. I heard the AI and neural-network testing is going well. How are the cognitive algorithms coming along?

Ken: Hi, Alex. We've been developing some advanced interfaces that are showing smoother robot interactions. The logic for AI intelligence is also showing some solid potential.

Alex: Impressive. Are we keeping up with ethical and industry compliance considerations?

Ken: Absolutely. We're syncing with the ethics committee to ensure the new AI applications meet ethical standards and focusing on encryption for IP protection and compliance.

Alex: Great. With the upcoming exhibitions, how are we planning to showcase these innovations?

Ken: The team is preparing an information brief highlighting our latest advancements in AI and neural networks. I will demonstrate two strategic solutions along with our final release plans.

Alex: Great! I'm working closely with the sales and marketing teams to leverage our branding strategy and keep our campaigns engaging. Your team's progress in AI and robotics development is key to market traction.

Ken: Agreed. Speaking of sales, we're also enhancing customer service feedback through a new AI chatbot. This should bolster analytics and overall conversion rates according to some tests we have been running.

Alex: Awesome! That's great to hear, Ken. Keep me updated on developments, especially those impacting key delivery deadlines.

Ken: Will do, Alex. The team is dedicated to pushing boundaries and we are all excited about bringing our new products to market.

Comprehension questions

Q1   What is the main focus of Ken and Alex's discussion?

Q2   How are the cognitive algorithms progressing according to Ken?

Q3   What is the team's approach to addressing ethical considerations in AI?

Q4   What is Ken's plan for showcasing their AI innovations?

Answer key p.116

ENGLISH AT THE SPEED OF TECH

UNIT | 08 AI and Robotics

PHRASE BANK

The phrases below will help you communicate more effectively about AI and Robotics. They cover a range of situations, from updating on project progress to discussing the ethical implications of AI. Use them to talk about projects, present your company's products, and address challenges and strategies. They will help you to convey complex AI concepts and articulate your ideas and recommendations with clarity and impact in a professional setting.

Updating on Progress
Our team's progress in ... includes ...
Our ongoing work focuses on ...
We have made significant gains in ...
We have been exploring ...

Discussing Ethical Considerations
We are ensuring ethics compliance by ...
The ethics committee is recommending ...
We're maintaining ethical standards by ...
Ethical considerations for AI involve ...

Planning and Strategizing
So we can ... , we are exploring ...
Strategies include ... and ...
We are working on ... so that we can ...
Future plans involve ... in order to ...

Making Recommendations
At first, I suggest focusing on ...
I would recommend ... to improve ...
Our team proposes ... in order to ...
I'd recommend ... so that we can ...

Highlighting Achievements
Thanks to ..., we're very happy to ...
Based on ..., we're thrilled to ...
With recent success in ..., we're ready to ...
A recent breakthrough now allows us to ...

Sharing Technical Insights
Our neural ... are more accurately ...
We've reduced AI ... errors by ...
Our updated ... are increasing ...
Personalized AI ... are ...

Problem-Solving and Adaptation
Our solution to ... is ...
Our revised ... strategy includes ...
We are applying adaptive processes to ...
Our adaptive approach to ... includes ...

Engaging in Team Discussions
Can we discuss how the ... are coming along?
If possible, I'd like some input on ...
What solutions do we have for ...?
Can we share some ideas about ..., please.

Communicating Future Plans
As promised, the .... will be ready by ...
As discussed, our team will ...
Following up, I will ... before ...
As planned, the ... will be completed by ...

Expressing Commitment
We're dedicated to pushing boundaries in ...
We're committed to deliver top-notch ...
We are always striving to innovate in ...
Our efforts are fully geared towards ...

CULTURE TIP

"In the fast-paced world of AI and robotics, clear communication and an open mind are key. Share your ideas openly and welcome new perspectives with enthusiasm. This team approach not only broadens our understanding of emerging technologies but also creates a supportive atmosphere for innovation. Encouraging each other's ideas leads to better strategies and breakthroughs, keeping everyone ahead in an ever-changing tech landscape."

ENGLISH AT THE SPEED OF TECH

UNIT 08 AI and Robotics

GRAMMAR FOCUS: PRESENT PERFECT CONTINUOUS

The present perfect continuous tense is key for highlighting work that has been ongoing and is still in progress, often focusing on the duration of the action. For example, "We have been implementing new updates since June." This tense is especially suitable for projects and other initiatives that require sustained effort and time. It helps to provide a sense of continuity and progress, reflecting a commitment to ongoing work and development.

1. We **have been improving** our AI algorithms continuously for the past few weeks.

2. Our engineers **have been testing** the new robotics software for almost a month.

3. The department **has been focusing** on AI-driven solutions for the last quarter.

> **Tip: The 'Have-Has Been, Resulting Effect' Rule for Present Perfect Continuous**
>
> ***Have-Has Been for Ongoing Actions:*** Use 'have been' or 'has been' + '-ing' form for actions that started in the past and continue into the present.
> Example: "She has been programming the new AI interface since last month."
> ***Resulting Effect for Outcomes:*** Also use this tense to show the current result or cause/effect of ongoing actions.
> Example: "The team is exhausted because they've been troubleshooting the network all night."

Unit 8 Task 5

GRAMMAR PRACTICE

Using the *Have-Has Been, Resulting Effect* rule for Present Perfect Continuous, look at the sentences below and decide which one of the two apply and then underline the relevant part(s) of the sentence. The first one is done for you.

1. (**Outcome**) <u>Productivity has increased</u> since we <u>have been automating</u> routine tasks.

2. (. . . . . .) Our chatbot has been learning to better interact with customers.

3. (. . . . . .) Our system's intelligence has been improving with ongoing analysis.

4. (. . . . . .) We have been iterating the logic behind our AI for better responses.

5. (. . . . . .) He's tired because he has been solving complex cognitive algorithms.

6. (. . . . . .) The team has been enhancing the neural network for improved data.

7. (. . . . . .) Customer satisfaction has grown as our AI has been refined.

8. (. . . . . .) The company's ethics have been evolving through ongoing discussions.

9. (. . . . . .) Engineers have been updating the new robot to enhance its functionality.

10. (. . . . . .) Designers have been streamlining the interface to make it intuitive

Answer key p.116

ENGLISH AT THE SPEED OF TECH

UNIT 08 AI and Robotics

GRAMMAR IN ACTION: AI AND ROBOTICS UPDATE

Scenario: As a team leader in the AI and Robotics department of a tech company, your task is to update your manager on the ongoing AI projects.

Prepare the Update: Write a brief overall report on the team's activities in the past week using the present perfect continuous tense to describe ongoing projects

Key Actions: Highlight actions related to developing AI logic, enhancing neural networks, and creating user-friendly AI interfaces.

Challenges and Solutions: Mention any challenges the team faced and the steps taken to address them.

Future Plans: Conclude with an overview of upcoming tasks, using future continuous tense for forward-looking statements.

Overall: ....

....

....

....

Key Actions: ....

....

....

....

Challenges and Solutions: ....

....

....

Future Plans: ....

....

....

Answer key p.116

ENGLISH AT THE SPEED OF TECH

UNIT | 08 AI and Robotics

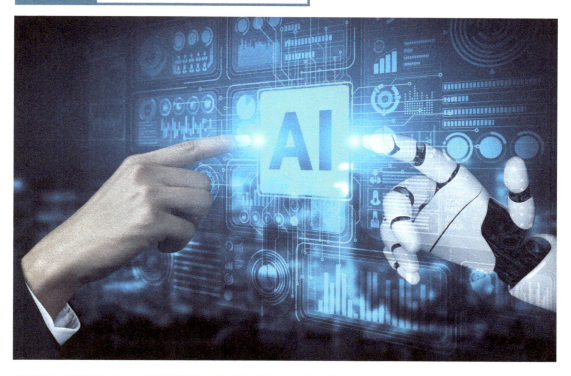

EXPANSION ACTIVITY: ROLE-PLAY/SIMULATION

In this role-play, you'll participate in an AI integration meeting between Alex, the AI Project Manager, and Jamie, the Lead AI Engineer. The discussion will revolve around the progress and challenges in integrating advanced neural networks into new robot designs, focusing on AI logic improvements and upcoming real-world testing. Use the provided prompts to steer your conversation, making use of the present perfect continuous tense to highlight ongoing developments and the future continuous tense for forthcoming tasks. This role-play is designed to help develop your skills for reporting, problem-solving, and future planning. A model dialogue is also included for reference.

> **TEACHER NOTES:** *Expansion activities can be more effective when done with a partner, allowing you to practice the language and skills learned in this lesson more fully. If you don't have a teacher, consider practicing with a colleague or friend. Online teachers and tutors are also available at very reasonable rates these days. If you would like teacher notes to support your learning journey, just send an email to* ***prospeak.author@outlook.com****, and we'll be happy to send you a PDF containing additional task notes, example responses, and expansion activity guidelines.*

ENGLISH AT THE SPEED OF TECH

UNIT 08 AI and Robotics

Role A

Role: Alex - AI Project Manager

AI Integration Meeting

Background

As the AI Project Manager, you're in charge of integrating advanced neural networks into the company's newest robot designs. Your team's focus has been on enhancing robots' decision-making abilities and human interaction capabilities, with a recent breakthrough in AI logic showing substantial improvements in both areas. The project has entered a critical phase where real-world testing is about to begin, and your goal is to ensure the robots perform effectively in a diverse range of environments.

Prompts

Share AI Logic Breakthrough: Discuss the recent breakthrough in AI logic, emphasizing its impact on decision-making in robots and potential applications across various industries.

Outline Real-World Testing Plans: Detail the upcoming real-world testing phase, specifying environments for testing and anticipated results.

Address Robotic Task Management: Talk about how the robots are equipped to handle complex tasks in dynamic settings, addressing any related concerns.

Plan Tech Exhibition Presentation: Propose concepts for a tech exhibition presentation that showcases the robots' advanced features.

NOTES

ENGLISH AT THE SPEED OF TECH

UNIT | **08 AI and Robotics**

Role B	Role: **Jamie - Lead AI Engineer**

AI Integration Meeting

Background

As the Lead AI Engineer, you've been hands-on with developing AI interfaces and working on neural network integration. Your recent work has focused on creating AI systems that can adapt to real-world situations, ensuring that the robots are not only technically proficient but also user-friendly and responsive to human commands. You have been closely involved in the design and testing of these systems, and you are keen to discuss their practical applications.

Prompts

Detail AI Interface Design: Explain the design aspects of AI interfaces, with a focus on user adaptability and functionality in diverse scenarios.

Share Preliminary Test Insights: Provide insights from preliminary tests, particularly how the robots have adapted to various commands and environments.

Discuss Testing Challenges and Solutions: Explore potential challenges expected in the real-world testing and propose strategies to overcome them.

Suggest AI System Enhancements: Recommend additional features or improvements for the AI systems, drawing from your experience in development and testing.

ENGLISH AT THE SPEED OF TECH

ROLE-PLAY/SIMULATION - SAMPLE DIALOGUE

Alex: Good morning, Jamie. I'm excited to discuss our breakthrough in AI logic in the latest robot interface iterations.

Jamie: *Morning, Alex. Absolutely, the integration of neural networks has really improved the robots' cognitive functions. Our tests show they're adapting well to varied commands in simulated environments.*

Alex: That's fantastic to hear. Regarding our real-world testing, what environments are we considering, and what outcomes are we expecting?

Jamie: *We're planning to test in both controlled lab settings and dynamic real-world scenarios. The goal is to ensure the robots can handle complex tasks and respond effectively to unpredictable elements.*

Alex: Perfect. We need to address any potential concerns about their performance in these environments. Also, for the tech exhibition, I'm thinking that we will showcase these advanced capabilities.

Jamie: *Great. I suggest we also focus on the user-friendly aspect of our AI interfaces during the demo. It's crucial we highlight their adaptability.*

Alex: Agreed. A live demo coupled with an interactive presentation should effectively showcase our progress. And on the enhancement front, what additional features do you think we could add?

Jamie: *I think adding more nuanced human interaction capabilities could be a game-changer. It'll make our robots even more relatable and versatile.*

Alex: Excellent idea. Let's develop that further. Thanks for your insights, Jamie.

Jamie: *Glad to help, Alex. I'm looking forward to seeing our plans come to market!*

Expansion - Report on AI Integration in Your Tech Environment

Write a report on how AI has been integrated into your current tech work. You should:

Begin with an overview of the any projects you've been using AI to help you with.

Detail ongoing processes, mentioning how AI has been enhancing these areas, using the present perfect continuous tense whenever possible.

• Discuss any challenges faced during integration and the strategies used to address them.

• Highlight the benefits and improvements AI has brought to your work environment.

• Conclude with future prospects or next steps in AI integration within your projects.

Focus on making your report reflective and analytical, showcasing how AI integration has been evolving and impacting your work. This task can be done individually or with a partner/teacher for feedback, enhancing your understanding and ability to communicate complex tech concepts. Good luck!

ENGLISH AT THE SPEED OF TECH

KEY VOCABULARY IN CONTEXT

Q1: We have been using disruptive logic **to** *interface* **with AI and robots.**

Incorrect: b) escalate is a verb, not a noun as is needed here.

Incorrect: c) iterate is a verb, not a noun.

Q2: Engineers have been trying to interact **with AI using** *responsive* **parameters.**

Incorrect: a) campaign can be used as a verb, but does not fit this context.

Incorrect: b) patent can be used as a verb, but does not fit this context.

Q3: The team has been studying neural **networks to enhance** *encryption*.

Incorrect: a) metrics is a noun, not an adjective as is needed here.

Incorrect: c) streamline is a verb, not an adjective.

Q4: The robot **has been navigating the research area without human** *input*.

Incorrect: a) pitch can be used as a noun, but does not fit this context.

Incorrect: c) escalate is a verb, not a noun as is needed here.

Q5: Researchers have been exploring cognitive **AI to improve** *campaign* **strategies.**

Incorrect: a) clarify is a verb, not an adjective as is needed here.

Incorrect: b) monetize is a verb, not an adjective.

Q6: We have been using code and logic as an interface **to robotic** *solutions*.

Incorrect: b) escalate is a verb, not a noun as is needed here.

Incorrect: c) innovate is a verb, not a noun.

Q7: Our team has been using artificial intelligence **to enhance** *predictive* **analytics.**

Incorrect: a) monetize is a verb, not a noun as is needed here.

Incorrect: b) escalate is a verb, not a noun.

Q8: We have been discussing ethics **in AI to align with our business** *strategy*.

Incorrect: b) launch is typically a verb, not a noun as is needed here.

Incorrect: c) debug is a verb, not a noun.

Q9: Our QA team has been working to automate **processes that** *validate* **data sets.**

Incorrect: a) solution is a noun, not a verb as is needed here.

Incorrect: b) confidential is an adjective, not a verb.

Q10: The design team has been using AI **to** *iterate* **prototyping procedures.**

Incorrect: a) persuade is a verb, not a noun as is needed here.

Incorrect: c) strategic is an adjective, not a noun.

NOTE: words in sentences 1-10 in *italics* are spaced repetition key words from previous units.

ENGLISH AT THE SPEED OF TECH

UNIT 08 Answer Key

BUSINESS DIALOGUE COMPREHENSION

Q1: What is the main focus of Ken and Alex's discussion?
• *Developments in AI and robotics, neural network testing, and compliance.*
Rationale: The dialogue revolves around updates and advancements in these areas.

Q2: How are the cognitive algorithms progressing according to Ken?
• *They are progressing well, especially for robot interactions.*
Rationale: Ken mentions advanced interfaces are enhancing robot interactions.

Q3: What is the team's approach to addressing ethical considerations in AI?
• *Collaborate with the ethics committee to ensure they meet ethical standards.*
Rationale: Ken discusses collaboration with the ethics committee.

Q4: What is Ken's plan for showcasing their AI innovations?
• *An informative brief highlighting AI advancements for upcoming exhibitions.*
Rationale: Ken talks about preparing a brief, as well as a demo to show scalability.

GRAMMAR PRACTICE

1. (**Outcome**) Productivity <u>has increased since</u> we <u>have been automating</u> routine tasks.

2. (**Ongoing**) Our chatbot <u>has been learning</u> to better interact with customers.

3. (**Outcome**) Our system's intelligence <u>has been improving</u> <u>with ongoing analysis</u>.

4. (**Ongoing**) We <u>have been iterating</u> the logic behind our AI for better responses.

5. (**Outcome**) <u>He's tired</u> because he <u>has been solving</u> complex cognitive algorithms.

6. (**Ongoing**) The team <u>has been enhancing</u> the neural network for improved data.

7. (**Outcome**) <u>Customer satisfaction has grown</u> as our <u>AI has been refined</u>.

8. (**Outcome**) The company's <u>ethics have been evolving</u> through <u>ongoing discussions</u>.

9. (**Ongoing**) Engineers <u>have been updating</u> the new robot to enhance its functionality.

10. (**Ongoing**) Designers <u>have been streamlining</u> the interface to make it intuitive.

GRAMMAR IN ACTION: AI AND ROBOTICS UPDATE

Example model answer:

Hi Jun,

I hope this message finds you well. Here's a quick update on our team's progress:

AI Logic and Neural Network Development: *We've been enhancing* AI logic and neural networks, aiming to create more intuitive interactions between our AI systems and users. This is crucial for advancing our robotics projects.

Interface Improvement and Analysis: Our engineers *have been focusing on* upgrading the AI interfaces, ensuring they are more user-friendly and efficient.

Challenges and Solutions: Although we encountered some hurdles with system integration, we *have been successfully implementing* solutions that have improved overall functionality.

Looking Ahead: Next week, we'll be concentrating on fine-tuning our AI algorithms and starting to integrate these advancements into our current robotics projects.

Let me know if you have any questions or suggestions.

Cheers!

Paulo

Tech Team Lead Engineer

Unit 08 Notes

....
....
....
....
....
....
....
....

Key takeaways

....
....
....
....

Useful Vocabulary

Use the text boxes below to write the word or phrase on the left and how it was used on the right.

Key words	Example sentence

Useful phrases	Example sentence

ENGLISH AT THE SPEED OF TECH

UNIT | 09 The Future of Tech

LEARNING OBJECTIVES

Welcome to Unit 9: The Future of Tech.
This unit introduces you to the language of future technology trends and predictions. You'll learn important terms and concepts about upcoming tech changes, as well as practicing the future perfect tense for talking about where technology might be heading. This unit is designed to build your communication skills for discussing future technology scenarios. Get ready to explore the possibilities that lie ahead in the tech world, preparing you for conversations about the exciting future of Global Tech.

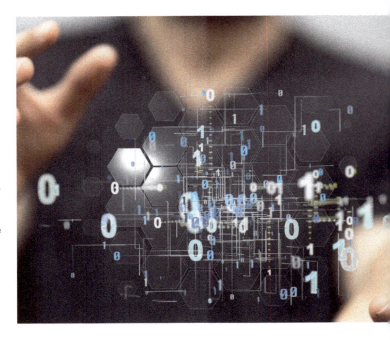

WARM-UP

Before starting the unit activities for "The Future of Tech," consider these questions to set the context for our lesson. Thinking about them will help lay the groundwork for what we will cover regarding future technology trends and developments. Note down your thoughts, as they will be useful to refer back to as we progress through the unit:

- What new disruptive technology do you expect to see go mainstream in the next 3-5 years?
- How do you think AI will impact the tech landscape and the way forward with new technology and ideas?

DID YOU KNOW...

"... that the pace at which human knowledge doubles has been accelerating at an astonishing rate? Pre-1900s, it was estimated to double each century. By the 1980s, this rate had increased to 18 months due to the introduction of the PC. In the early 2000s, with the internet and big data, human knowledge started doubling every couple of months, and now, with advancements in AI and machine learning, some suggest it is doubling every 12 hours! Looking forward, experts predict that the continuous evolution of AI and quantum computing will allow knowledge doubling to occur almost in real-time!"

ENGLISH AT THE SPEED OF TECH

UNIT | 09 The Future of Tech

KEY VOCABULARY IN CONTEXT

futuristic (adj), quantum computing (n), integrate (v), VR (n), evolve (v), sustainable (adj), innovate (v), biotech (n), cloud computing (n), wearables (n)

Read this memo to see the key words used in a Future Vision context.

MEMO: Embracing Our *Futuristic* Vision in Tech

To: All Employees

Dear Team,

I'm thrilled to share our strategic vision for the future as we *integrate* cutting-edge technologies like *quantum computing*, *VR*, and *cloud computing* into our core operations. We're focusing on developing sustainable and futuristic solutions, integrating *wearables* and *biotech* innovations that resonate with our core principles and ethical commitments.

Significant progress has been made in AI as our cognitive interfaces and neural algorithms redefine user experiences. By next year, we anticipate these AI-driven platforms will revolutionize customer engagement, making interactions more personalized and intuitive than ever.

We're also seeking strategic collaborations to enhance our quantum computing capabilities, boosting data processing power to support our cutting-edge technology. Our cloud computing infrastructure is also *evolving* to be more secure and scalable.

As we move forward, our strength lies in our ability to *innovate* and adapt. Our branding and campaign strategies will reflect this dynamic approach, capturing our transformative journey in tech.

Thank you for your dedication. Together, we're shaping a *sustainable* and technologically advanced future.

Best regards,

Roland Mehta, CEO

PRO-TIP: Boost your technical English vocabulary with 'multimedia learning'. Explore tech-focused videos, podcasts, and webinars, and note useful words and, phrases. Record these in a vocabulary notebook, including context and usage. Regular review and usage in conversations or writing will improve retention and understanding. This approach not only enriches your technical lexicon but also improves your fluency and comprehension in English.

ENGLISH AT THE SPEED OF TECH

UNIT 09 The Future of Tech

KEY VOCABULARY IN CONTEXT - PRACTICE

Complete the sentences below by filling in each blank with the best word from the choices provided. The first one is done for you.

1.   By next year, our . . . . designs will have *streamlined* all user interfaces.

A. escalate	**B. futuristic**	C. iterate

2.   We will have integrated . . . . into our *encryption* protocols by next year.

A. disrupt innovate	B. iterate logic	C. quantum computing

3.   Our developers will have . . . . AI into our *network* systems by December.

A. sponsor	B. integrated	C. campaign

4.   By Q4, ... technology will have *revolutionized* our training methodology.

A. VR	B. monetize	C. encrypt

5.   Our software will have. . . . . to provide *responsive* feedback by year end.

A. campaign	B. iterate	C. evolved

6.   By 2027, we will have . . . . solutions *interfacing* with smart cities.

A. sustainable	B. disrupt	C. iterate

7.   By next week, we will have . . . . new *strategies* for tech products.

A. innovated	B. panel	C. encrypt

8.   Our . . . . team will have *encrypted* crucial data by the end of this month.

A. automate	B. iterate	C. biotech

9.   Our . . . . infrastructure will have *secured* all data by next month.

A. disrupt persuade	B. AI monitor	C. cloud computing

10.   All employees will have *tested* the latest health . . . . by year-end.

A. wearables	B. validate	C. protect

Answer key p.129

ENGLISH AT THE SPEED OF TECH

UNIT 09 The Future of Tech

BUSINESS DIALOGUE

Read the dialogue and answer the comprehension questions that follow below.

Tina: Hi Alex, following up on Roland's recent Tech Brief, how's the AI integration project coming along?

Alex: Hey Tina. Good. We've been aligning AI with quantum computing to evolve our neural interfaces. We'll have automated most key processes by the end of Q3.

Tina: Sounds promising. Integrating quantum computing with cloud computing and VR is crucial for a sustainable tech vision. We're hoping to see some innovative new products come to market this year.

Alex: Absolutely. The integration's impact on biotech and wearables will be transformative. Gains in these areas will reshape user experience in all of our new products.

Tina: Roland also emphasized the importance of effective branding. We need to launch a strategic campaign showcasing these futuristic solutions soon.

Alex: Right, our next meetings should focus on how this technology potentially interacts with different sectors.

Tina: Right. Demoing some of our AI-driven wearables at the upcoming tech exhibitions will be a game-changer for us. It will showcase our cutting-edge technology even more effectively.

Alex: For sure. The team is working hard on models for these AI integrations. We aim to demo solutions that can adapt to evolving market needs.

Tina: Great! Leveraging our expertise in quantum computing and AI, I'm sure we can set a new benchmark in this technology.

Alex: Definitely. These innovations are a huge plus for our company's future.

Comprehension questions

Q1 What is the main focus of the AI integration project led by Alex?

Q2 How does Tina describe the importance of integrating quantum computing with other technologies?

Q3 What impact is expected from the integration of AI in wearables?

Q4 What are Alex and Tina's plans for the upcoming exhibitions?

Answer key p.130

ENGLISH AT THE SPEED OF TECH

UNIT | 09 The Future of Tech

PHRASE BANK

The phrases below will help you discuss tech integrations and impacts more effectively. They cover scenarios from setting project milestones to justifying investments and predicting business impacts. Adapt them to articulate your strategic plans, evaluate potential benefits, and communicate your vision for integrating advanced technologies. Doing so will enhance your ability to convey complex future-focused concepts and articulate strategic initiatives with clarity and impact.

Discussing Future Integrations
By ..., we will have fully integrated ...
The team will have secured ... before ...
Cloud computing will have enhanced ... by ...
VR training will have been adopted by ...

Predicting Technological Impacts
AI will have transformed ... by ...
Wearables will have enhanced ... by ...
Biotech gains will have improved ... by ...
Augmented reality will have altered ... by ...

Setting Project Milestones
By the project's third phase, we will have ...
Our ... will have been launched by ...
Key milestones will have been achieved by ...
We will have finalized ... by ...

Exploring Strategic Collaborations
We will have partnered with ... by ...
Collaboration will have been agreed by ...
Key partners will have been decided by ...
Alliances will have been identified by ...

Evaluating Efficiency Gains
Before ..., we will have reduced ...
Our ... will have increased by leveraging ...
... will have been minimized before ...
... efficiency will have increased by ...

Justifying Technology Investments
Investing in ... is justified through ...
The ... will have been validated by ...
Our investment in ... will have reduced ...
... resources will have been optimized by ...

Managing Change and Innovation
By adopting ..., we will have achieved ...
Our ... will have significant impact on ...
Changes in ... will have been finalized by ...
... innovations ... will have been done by ...

Improving Product Offerings
By refining ..., we will have enhanced ...
Our ... will have been expanded by ...
... quality will have been improved by ...
... satisfaction will have been gained by ...

Enhancing Data Security
Before upgrading ..., we will have ...
Security in ... will have been tightened by ...
... compliance will have been set by ...
Protocols for ... will have been revised by ...

Fostering Sustainability Practices
Before ..., we will have reduced waste by ...
Sustainable ... will have been adopted by ...
Sourcing of ... will have been agreed by ...
... will have been demonstrated by ...

CULTURE TIP

"Working with global teams means understanding different ways of communicating. For example, in Asia and the Middle East, people often imply things rather than say them directly — they tend to use more than just words to get their point across. In Europe and North America, people usually like to communicate in a straightforward way, saying exactly what they mean. Knowing this can help teams work together and understand each other more smoothly."

ENGLISH AT THE SPEED OF TECH

UNIT | 09 The Future of Tech

GRAMMAR FOCUS: FUTURE PERFECT

The Future Perfect tense is critical for discussing outcomes that need to be completed before a specific point in the future. This tense is particularly relevant in the fast-evolving tech industry, where setting clear targets for project completions is essential for strategic planning. By including the Future Perfect in project updates, you can more effectively communicate about developments that will have been completed by future deadlines, setting clear expectations for future milestones.

1. By next year, **we will have integrated** quantum computing into our database operations.

2. Our team **will have enhanced** the VR capabilities of the new product by next quarter.

3. We **will have finalized** our cybersecurity protocols before the system audit.

> ### Tip: The 'By and Before' Rule for Future Perfect
> ***By for Deadlines:*** Use the Future Perfect with 'by' to discuss deadlines.
> Example: "By the end of the quarter, we will have launched the new app."
> ***Before for Priority:*** Use 'before' to indicate an action that will be completed before another event.
> Example: "We will have completed the system update before moving to the new data center."

Unit 9 Task 5

GRAMMAR PRACTICE

Using the **'By and Before'** rule for future Perfect, look at the sentences below and decide which one of the two apply and then underline the relevant part(s) of the sentence. The first one is done for you.

1. (Before) Encryption <u>will have improved</u> <u>before</u> integrating the new software.

2. (. . . . . .) We will have patented our biotech technology ...... the end of this quarter.

3. (. . . . . .) We will have moved to cloud computing ...... upgrading the server.

4. (. . . . . .) Prototyping will have evolved to beta version two ...... the end of this week.

5. (. . . . . .) Quantum computing will have analyzed the data ...... the audit begins.

6. (. . . . . .) Our futuristic design will have expanded market share ...... the launch date.

7. (. . . . . .) We will have set-up sustainable practices ...... revising guidelines.

8. (. . . . . .) We will have innovated our R&D approach ...... the end of this year.

9. (. . . . . .) Our software will have improved the UX on our wearables ...... June.

10. (. . . . . .) VR will have improved training outcomes ...... updating our systems.

Answer key p.130

ENGLISH AT THE SPEED OF TECH

UNIT | 09 The Future of Tech

GRAMMAR IN ACTION: TECHNOLOGY INTEGRATION PROPOSAL

Objective: Use the Future Perfect tense to outline key outcomes of integrating a new technology into a company project.

Scenario: As team members of a dynamic tech company, you are tasked with drafting a proposal to integrate one of the cutting-edge technologies—quantum computing, VR, or cloud computing—into an existing project of your choice. This proposal will outline how this integration will contribute to the company's operations and strategic goals.

Instructions: Begin by re-reading the CEO's recent email to all employees, which outlines the company's futuristic vision and mentions specific technologies (Unit 9 Task 2). This email will serve as a foundation for understanding the strategic importance and potential impact of the technology you choose.

Choose a Technology: Select one of the technologies mentioned in the CEO's email (quantum computing, VR, or cloud computing). Consider how this technology can be applied to enhance a current project or operation within the company.

Draft Your Proposal

Introduction: Briefly describe the chosen technology and the project it will be integrated with.

Body: Using the Future Perfect tense, detail the outcomes that will have been achieved by integrating this technology by the end of the fiscal year. Focus on the anticipated benefits such as improved efficiency, enhanced user experience, increased productivity, etc.

Conclusion: Summarize the expected impact of the technology integration on the project and the overall strategic goals of the company.

Submission: Submit your proposal to the course teacher or a peer for feedback.

Optional: Prepare a short presentation to your teacher or a peer and be sure to highlight the use of the Future Perfect tense to set clear expectations for future milestones.

Answer key p.130

ENGLISH AT THE SPEED OF TECH

UNIT | 09 The Future of Tech

EXPANSION ACTIVITY: ROLE-PLAY/SIMULATION

In this role-play, you'll simulate a strategic planning meeting between Teri, the Tech Strategy Manager, and Lee, the Innovation Development Leader. The discussion will focus on the integration of emerging technologies such as quantum computing, VR, and cloud computing into the company's existing projects. The dialogue will explore how these technologies will be utilized to achieve strategic objectives, enhance operational efficiency, and meet future market demands. Use the provided prompts to guide your conversation, employing the Future Perfect tense to discuss the anticipated completions of technology integration and their impact on the company's strategic goals. A model dialogue is also included for reference.

TEACHER NOTES: *Expansion activities can be more effective when done with a partner, allowing you to practice the language and skills learned in this lesson more fully. If you don't have a teacher, consider practicing with a colleague or friend. Online teachers and tutors are also available at very reasonable rates these days. If you would like teacher notes to support your learning journey, just send an email to **prospeak.author@outlook.com**, and we'll be happy to send you a PDF containing additional task notes, example responses, and expansion activity guidelines.*

ENGLISH AT THE SPEED OF TECH

UNIT 09 The Future of Tech

Role A	Role: **Teri - Tech Strategy Manager**

Tech Integration: Strategic Alignment Meeting

Background

As the Tech Strategy Manager, you oversee strategic planning for technology integration across company projects. With the company's move towards adopting more advanced technologies like quantum computing and VR, you are tasked with outlining how these technologies will be integrated into different sectors of the company. Your goal is to ensure that these integrations are aligned with the company's long-term strategic goals.

Prompts

Outline Integration Goals: Discuss how quantum computing will have been integrated into data security by the end of the fiscal year.

Evaluate Tech Impact: Explain how VR technology will have transformed the training programs, particularly focusing on employee performance and engagement.

Assess Future Milestones: Project how the adoption of cloud computing will have optimized the company's infrastructure for scalability and security by next quarter.

Strategize Upcoming Projects: Plan which technologies will have been adopted in new market segments and their expected impact on the company's growth.

NOTES

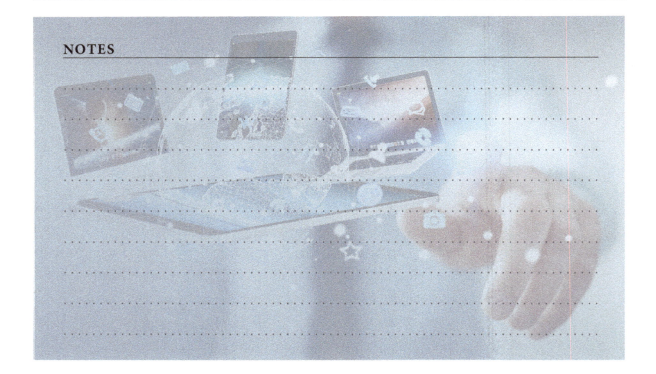

ENGLISH AT THE SPEED OF TECH

UNIT | 09 The Future of Tech

Role B

Role: Lee - Innovation Development Leader

Tech Integration: Strategic Alignment Meeting

Background

As the Innovation Development Leader, you are responsible for the implementation and management of new tech projects. Your role involves closely working with different department heads to ensure the technology integration is smooth and meets operational needs. You also monitor the progress and effectiveness of these integrations.

Prompts

Discuss Implementation Strategies: Share how AI and quantum computing will have enhanced analytical capabilities across business operations.

Review Tech Advancements: Reflect on how the integration of cloud computing will have increased overall operational efficiency and data management by the year's end.

Highlight Technological Achievements: Mention specific projects where VR will have boosted client interaction and sales presentations.

Future Tech Forecasts: Suggest further technological advancements that will have been explored to keep the company at the forefront of innovation.

ENGLISH AT THE SPEED OF TECH

UNIT | 09 The Future of Tech

ROLE-PLAY/SIMULATION - SAMPLE DIALOGUE

Teri: Hi Lee. I'm happy to report that by the end of this quarter we will have fully integrated VR into our customer service platforms. How do you see this impacting our client interactions?

Lee: *Hi Teri. That's great! With VR, we will have created a more immersive experience, enhancing customer satisfaction significantly. We're also planning to roll out VR training for all our support staff.*

Teri: Sounds promising. With regards to progress with our quantum computing platform, will we have resolved the integration challenges with our existing data systems by next month?

Lee: *There are still some hurdles, but we will have developed a more robust integration protocol to ensure functionality between our quantum systems and traditional databases by then.*

Teri: Excellent! And what about the cloud computing enhancements? By the end of Q3, will we have improved our infrastructure to handle increased data loads.

Lee: *Absolutely, we will have upgraded our servers and cloud capabilities, which will improve processing power and data storage significantly.*

Teri: Great! Let's be sure to stay well ahead of the curve. Can we discuss this further and outline steps more concretely in our next meeting?

Lee: *Sure. I'll prepare a detailed forecast of our tech upgrades and how they align with our strategic goals. How's next Wednesday for a deep dive?*

Teri: Perfect, Lee. I'll send out the invite and an agenda by tomorrow.

Lee: *Looking forward to it! I think these upgrades will set a new standard in our industry.*

Expansion - Tech Integration Strategy

Develop a strategic plan for integrating a technology like blockchain, augmented reality, or next-generation AI into your operations. Using the Future Perfect tense, outline the integration's objectives and time lines, for example, "By Q3 next year, we will have fully integrated blockchain to enhance transaction security." You should focus on:

Milestones: Key targets and their completion dates.

Benefits: Expected advantages, such as increased efficiency.

Challenges: Potential obstacles and planned resolutions.

Practice: Deliver your strategy in a concise 3-minute presentation. Aim to clearly articulate complex integration plans using the Future Perfect tense. This can be done individually or with feedback from your teacher or peers for improvement. Good luck!

ENGLISH AT THE SPEED OF TECH

UNIT 09 Answer Key

KEY VOCABULARY IN CONTEXT

Q1: By next year, our futuristic designs will have *streamlined* all user interfaces.

Incorrect: a) escalate is a verb, not an adjective as is needed here.

Incorrect: c) iterate is a verb, not an adjective.

Q2: We will have integrated quantum computing into our *encryption* by next year.

Incorrect: a) 'disrupt innovate' is a nonsense compound noun.

Incorrect: b) 'iterate logic' is a nonsense compound noun.

Q3: Our developers will have integrated AI into our *network* systems by December.

Incorrect: a) sponsor can be used as a verb, but does not fit this context or tense.

Incorrect: c) campaign can be used as a verb, but does not fit this context or tense.

Q4: By Q4, VR technology will have *revolutionized* our training methodology.

Incorrect: b) monetize is a verb, not part of a compound noun as is needed here.

Incorrect: c) encrypt is a verb, not a noun.

Q5: Our software will have evolved to provide *responsive* feedback by year end.

Incorrect: a) campaign can be used as a verb, but does not fit this context or tense.

Incorrect: b) iterate is a verb, but does not fit this context or tense.

Q6: By 2027, we will have sustainable solutions *interfacing* with smart cities.

Incorrect: b) disrupt is a verb, not an adjective as is needed here.

Incorrect: c) iterate is a verb, not an adjective.

Q7: By next week, we will have innovated new *strategies* for tech products.

Incorrect: b) panel is a noun, not a verb as is needed here.

Incorrect: c) encrypt is a verb, but does not work in this context or tense.

Q8: Our biotech team will have *encrypted* crucial data by the end of this month.

Incorrect: a) automate is a verb, not an adjective as is needed here.

Incorrect: b) iterate is a verb, not an adjective.

Q9: Our cloud computing infrastructure will have secured data by next month.

Incorrect: a) 'disrupt persuade' is a nonsense compound noun.

Incorrect: b) 'AI monitor' is a nonsense compound noun.

Q10: All employees will have *tested* the latest health wearables by year-end.

Incorrect: b) validate is a verb, not a noun as is needed here.

Incorrect: c) protect is a verb, not a noun.

NOTE: words in sentences 1-10 in *italics* are spaced repetition key words from previous units.

ENGLISH AT THE SPEED OF TECH

UNIT 09 Answer Key

BUSINESS DIALOGUE COMPREHENSION

Q1: What is the main focus of the AI integration project led by Alex?
• *The main focus is on aligning AI with quantum computing to evolve neural interfaces and automate key processes by the end of Q3.*

Q2: How does Tina describe the importance of integrating quantum computing with other technologies?
• *Tina describes it as crucial for a sustainable tech vision and necessary for bringing innovative new products to market.*

Q3: What impact is expected from the integration of AI in biotech and wearables?
• *The integration is expected to be transformative, reshaping user experience in all of their new products.*

Q4: What are Alex and Tina's plans for the upcoming exhibitions?
• *They plan to showcase demo AI-driven wearables and showcase cutting-edge technology.*

GRAMMAR PRACTICE

1) **(Before)** Encryption will have improved before integrating the new software. *(ing verb)*

2) **(By)** We will have patented our biotech technology by the end of this quarter. *(time line)*

3) **(Before)** We will have moved to cloud computing before upgrading the server. *(ing verb)*

4) **(By)** Prototyping will have evolved to beta version two by the end of this week. *(time line)*

5) **(Before)** Quantum computing will have analyzed the data before the audit begins. *(ing verb)*

6) **(By)** Our futuristic design will have expanded market share by the launch date. *(time line)*

7) **(Before)** We will have implemented sustainable practices before revising guidelines. *(ing verb)*

8) **(By)** We will have innovated our R&D approach by the end of this year. *(time line)*

9) **(By)** Our software will have improved the UX on our wearables by June. *(time line)*

10) **(Before)** VR will have improved training outcomes before updating our systems. *(ing verb)*

GRAMMAR IN ACTION: TECHNOLOGY INTEGRATION PROPOSAL

Example model answer:

Technology Integration Proposal: Virtual Reality (VR) for Training Enhancement

Introduction: In alignment with our company's forward-looking strategy, this proposal recommends integrating Virtual Reality (VR) technology into our current training modules. This initiative aims to significantly enhance learning experiences and participant engagement across all departments.

Body: By the end of this fiscal year, we **will have transformed** our conventional training methodologies into an interactive VR-based learning environment. This shift **will have enabled** us to present complex information in an engaging and digestible format, resulting in higher retention rates. Additionally, we **will have streamlined** the onboarding process for new hires, integrating them more effectively into our operational workflow. The use of VR **will have also facilitated** more nuanced training scenarios that enhance decision-making and problem-solving skills in real-world settings.

Conclusion: The integration of VR technology into our training framework **will have solidified** our commitment to leveraging cutting-edge technology to drive educational excellence. This initiative not only aligns with our strategic goals of fostering innovation and efficiency but also ensures a state-of-the-art learning environment that propels our company ahead in the competitive tech industry.

Unit 09 Notes

....
....
....
....
....
....
....
....

Key takeaways

....
....
....
....

Useful Vocabulary

Use the text boxes below to write the word or phrase on the left and how it was used on the right.

Key words	Example sentence

Useful phrases	Example sentence

ENGLISH AT THE SPEED OF TECH

UNIT | 10 Effective Communication in Big Tech

LEARNING OBJECTIVES

Welcome to Unit 10: Effective Communication in Big Tech. This unit will help sharpen your ability to communicate information and ideas more effectively. We'll focus on why being clear, concise, and complete is crucial for conveying your message, as well as on using conditionals to describe processes and outcomes. You'll master the essential language needed to articulate business goals and project details to achieve desired outcomes. Prepare to elevate your professional communication skills, ensuring you can navigate and contribute to complex discussions in your field of expertise.

Unit 10 Task 1 ### WARM-UP

Before starting the unit on 'Effective Communication in Big Tech,' consider these questions to set some context for the lesson. Reflecting on them will lay the groundwork for the language and skills we will cover about effective communication strategies in Big Tech industry. Note down your thoughts to look back on as we go:

- How can clear stakeholder communication impact tech initiative outcomes?
- How can effective communication enhance collaboration with remote tech teams?

DID YOU KNOW...

"... that mastering business communication can transform your career? Top leaders like Jeff Bezos and Indra Nooyi emphasize its importance. Bezos banned PowerPoint at Amazon, insisting on narrative memos to enhance clarity. Nooyi, former CEO of PepsiCo, believes you can't over-invest in communication skills. Effective communication, from simple words to powerful metaphors, can significantly boost productivity, align teams, and inspire action. Surprisingly, writing in a way that's easy to read and understand, like using short words and clear metaphors, can make your message far more persuasive and memorable!" (HBR Nov. 2022)

ENGLISH AT THE SPEED OF TECH

UNIT 10 Effective Communication in Big Tech

KEY VOCABULARY IN CONTEXT

executive summary (n), articulate (v), complete (adj), action items (n), specific (adj), minutes (n), summarize (v), clear (adj), concise (adj), convey (v)

Read this Memo to see the key words used in an effective communication context.

MEMO

From: Bill Sabin, Director of Learning and Development

To: All Department Members

Dear Team,

As we continue to lead in the tech industry, our ability to communicate in a *clear*, *concise*, and *complete* manner remains paramount. Effective business communication not only *conveys* critical information but also influences project outcomes and stakeholder perceptions.

Tips for Effective Business Communication:

Be Clear and Concise: Strive to clearly and concisely convey your messages without sacrificing completeness.

Be Complete: Include all necessary information and details, ensuring nothing vital is omitted that would require follow-up questions.

Structure Your Message: Begin with an *executive summary* that *articulates* the core message clearly and concisely. Organize content with headings and bullet points for easier navigation.

Use *Action Items*: Assign action items clearly and include *specific* deadlines, if required. Use direct language so that everyone knows their roles and responsibilities.

Maintain Accurate Records: Keep the *minutes* of meetings concise, serving as a clear and reliable record of your meetings. Be sure to *summarize* key points and decisions clearly.

Revise and Proofread: Always review your documents for accuracy and clarity. Doing so ensures that all communications reflect our high standards and are free of errors.

Thank you for your commitment to excellence.

Best Regards,

Bill

PRO-TIP: Finding opportunities to engage in 'peer teaching' is an excellent way to deepen your understanding of new material, improve vocabulary recall, and promote collaborative learning within your professional community. Peer teaching can be as straightforward as explaining a new word, concept, or procedure to a colleague or classmate. Remember to invite questions and feedback during these teaching sessions. It's a win-win scenario—you'll not only reinforce your own knowledge but also boost your confidence as well.

ENGLISH AT THE SPEED OF TECH

UNIT 10 Effective Communication in Big Tech

KEY VOCABULARY IN CONTEXT - PRACTICE

Complete the sentences below by filling in each blank with the best word from the choices provided. The first one is done for you.

1. If we include an . . . . , it will provide a snapshot of our *strategic* direction.

A. algorithm	B. executive summary	C. interface

2. She effectively . . . . the project scope to *stakeholders* yesterday.

A. encrypted	B. monitored	C. articulated

3. Our team has been ensuring stakeholders get . . . . *updates* this quarter.

A. complete	B. clarify	C. monetize

4. If we set clear . . . . , everyone will know their *responsibilities*.

A. modularity	B. encryption	C. action items

5. Our team has been defining . . . . goals to improve *focus*.

A. encrypted	B. specific	C. monitored

6. Taking regular meeting. . . . . has helped *clarify* decision-making processes.

A. minutes	B. prototype	C. sponsorship

7. If you . . . . decisions and main ideas, we can ensure *consensus*.

A. traction	B. prototype	C. summarize

8. We have been *focusing* on . . . . communication to prevent misunderstandings.

A. automate	B. clear	C. iterate

9. Being clear and . . . . in her presentation helped win *stakeholder* approval.

A. scalable	B. concise	C. viral

10. If you can successfully . . . . the *benefits*, securing approval becomes easier.

A. interact	B. debug	C. convey

Answer key p.143

BUSINESS DIALOGUE

Read the dialogue and answer the comprehension questions that follow below.

Bill: Hi Linda, thanks for your time today. The stakeholder meeting is next week and our presentation needs to be a 'home run'. We'll definitely need to emphasize our strategic initiatives as effectively as we can.

Linda: Absolutely, Bill. An executive summary highlighting our main achievements and plans will help set the right tone. Then we can showcase our progress in quantum computing and sustainable practices.

Bill: Great. If we make sure each slide has concise headings and bullet points we can maintain clarity for more engagement. It's also key to make our recent achievements clear, concise, and complete.

Linda: I totally agree, Bill. I'll draft slides on our innovative approaches along with metrics for measuring success. If we have time, we can also include some key encryption enhancements and interface updates for our wearables.

Bill: Perfect, let's keep those points as streamlined as possible. For the Q&A, let's assign roles. We need to be prepared for any questions on network security updates and AI integration.

Linda: I'll coordinate with the tech team for the latest updates and prepare for potential questions. How about we rehearse next Thursday?

Bill: Thursday works. Let's keep refining our message to ensure it's impactful. This meeting influences our budget outcomes significantly. Thanks, Linda.

Linda: Thanks, Bill. I'll ensure everything's set for our rehearsal. We'll deliver a presentation that truly reflects our commitment to excellence.

Comprehension questions

Q1 What is the main purpose of the executive summary Linda plans to include?

Q2 Why is it important for each slide to have concise headings and bullet points according to Bill?

Q3 What additional content does Linda propose to include in the presentation if there is enough time?

Q4 What does Bill suggest to prepare for the Q&A session of the presentation?

Answer key p.144

UNIT | 10 Effective Communication in Big Tech

PHRASE BANK

The phrases below will help you discuss tech integrations and impacts more effectively. They cover scenarios from setting project milestones to justifying investments and predicting business impacts. Adapt them to articulate your strategic plans, evaluate potential benefits, and communicate your vision for integrating advanced technologies. Doing so will enhance your ability to convey complex future-focused concepts and articulate strategic initiatives with clarity and impact.

Starting a Conversation
Hi ..., thanks for meeting with me today.
Thanks for your time, ..., I'd like to discuss ...
Could we quickly go over ...
I like to catch up on progress with ...

Emphasizing Strategic Initiatives
We'll need to emphasize our ...
We need to highlight our key strategies in ...
Focusing on ... initiatives will help ...
Let's focus on our strategic direction by ...

Proposing Solutions and Ideas
What if we ..., doing so could ...
I was thinking we might ...
Perhaps we should consider ...
Couldn't we ... by ...?

Clarifying and Summarizing Points
To summarize, we agreed that ...
Let me clarify next steps for ...
In summary, we will focus on ...
Just to be clear, our objectives are ...

Providing Technical Updates
As requested, we just updated the ...
Our latest ... updates include ...
The ... updates are ready for ...
As planned, we've completed the ....

Being Well Prepared
We'll need to be prepared for ...
Let's plan for challenges such as ...
In case of unforeseen issues, we have to ...
We'll definitely need to consider ...

Assigning Roles and Responsibilities
I'd like to assign roles for ...
..., If possible, can you handle ..., please.
I'll take responsibility for ...
..., I'd like you to manage the ...

Encouraging Collaboration
Let's collaborate closely to ensure...
I'll coordinate with ... to ...
Your cooperation is crucial for ...
Let's work together to finalize ...

Finalizing Preparations
Great! So, our final step will be ...
I think we should ... just to make sure.
Finalizing ... will require us to ...
Our last step is to confirm that ... is ready.

Concluding Discussions
Thanks ... Your efforts have been ...
I appreciate your ..., let's wrap up by ...
Thanks for your hard work, ... Great job!
Let's conclude with a review of ...

CULTURE TIP

"Effective communication is crucial on global teams. Speak clearly to accommodate diverse language backgrounds, and listen attentively, showing respect for different opinions and viewpoints. Adapt to cultural communication styles—some may prefer directness, while others may favor a more relaxed approach. A respectful and inclusive environment enhances team morale and productivity, leading to greater success in multicultural team settings."

ENGLISH AT THE SPEED OF TECH

UNIT 10 Effective Communication in Big Tech

GRAMMAR FOCUS: CONDITIONALS

Conditionals are crucial for outlining potential outcomes. Phrases such as, "If we integrate this software, productivity will increase," clearly communicate hypothetical scenarios and their implications. This grammatical structure is invaluable for discussing technological integrations and planning under uncertainty, ensuring that global teams understand and effectively manage potential developments and changes.

1. **If we update the software**, system performance gain will be significant.

2. **If you reset your password,** access should be immediately restored.

3. **If we adopt a cloud storage back-up**, data loss is sure to decrease.

> ### Tip: The 'If, Unless, and When' Rule for Conditionals
>
> *If for Probability:* Use 'if' for potential outcomes based on specific conditions. Example: "If we integrate this API, our app's functionality will improve."
> *Unless for Exceptions:* Use 'unless' to highlight necessary conditions to prevent undesired outcomes. Example: "Unless we meet the deadline, we will face delays."
> *When for Certainty:* Use 'when' for situations where the outcome is certain once conditions are met. Example: "Once you submit the budget proposal, we will finalize the decision."

Unit 10 Task 5

GRAMMAR PRACTICE

Using the **'If, Unless, and When'** Rule for Conditionals rule, look at the sentences below and decide which one to apply *(Prob, Except, Cert)* and then add to and underline the relevant part(s) of the sentence. The first one is done for you.

1. (..**Except**..) ..Unless.. we secure more funding, project expansion <u>will be</u> cancelled.

2. (. . . . . .) .... we automate these tasks, overall efficiency will increase.

3. (. . . . . .) .... you complete the course, your skills will be updated.

4. (. . . . . .) .... we invest in AI, our data analysis will be faster.

5. (. . . . . .) .... we comply with regulations, penalties may be incurred.

6. (. . . . . .) .... we upgrade our servers, response times will improve.

7. (. . . . . .) .... we adopt blockchain, transaction security will be enhanced.

8. (. . . . . .) .... we finalize this deal, our market share will expand.

9. (. . . . . .) .... we update our software, system vulnerabilities will remain.

10. (. . . . . .) .... we train employees now, future performance will benefit.

Answer key p.144

ENGLISH AT THE SPEED OF TECH

UNIT | 10 Effective Communication in Big Tech

GRAMMAR IN ACTION: USING CONDITIONALS

Objective: Enhance your ability to use conditional statements more effectively in negotiation situations.

Activity: Think about various negotiation scenarios in which you might use conditional statements. This exercise will help you articulate terms, respond to offers, or address potential conflicts.

Instructions: Using the scenarios below, write responses using at least one conditional term. Aim to explore different outcomes based on the conditions you set.

SCENARIOS:

Contract Renewal: A vendor wants to increase service fees by 20%.
Example: *"If you keep the current fee, we can extend the contract for another two years."*
Yours: ....
Yours: ....

Upgrade Request: Your manager is hesitant to approve an upgrade request due to budget.
Example: *"Unless we make the hardware upgrade, uptime can't be guaranteed."*
Yours: ....

Yours: ....

Revision Requirement: A contractor is required to make a revision before payment.
Example: *"When the revisions meet product specs, your invoice will be processed."*
Yours: ....

Yours: ....

EXTENDED PRACTICE: Expand your skills with these additional scenarios:

Remote Work Agreement: Discussing terms for continuing to work remotely.
Example: *"If I continue to meet all performance targets, can I continue to work remotely?"*
Yours: ....

Salary Negotiation: Discussing a salary increase based on recent performance.
Example: *"If you approve a 10% raise, I can commit to leading two major projects."*
Yours: ....

Supplier Terms: Negotiating better terms with a supplier due to increased order volumes.
Example: *"If we double our order size, could you commit to a 15% discount?"*
Yours: ....

Answer key p.144

ENGLISH AT THE SPEED OF TECH

UNIT | 10 Effective Communication in Big Tech

EXPANSION ACTIVITY: ROLE-PLAY/SIMULATION

In this role-play, you'll take part in the pre-meeting between Bill, Director of Learning and Development, and Linda, Tech Team Manager before their stakeholder meeting. Prepare to finalize and rehearse a strategic presentation covering innovative initiatives like quantum computing and sustainable practices. Try to include the use of conditionals to explore hypothetical scenarios and articulate updates effectively using the provided prompts. This exercise is designed to sharpen your skills in effective communication, strategic planning, and collaborative problem-solving, preparing you for demanding business interactions and enhancing your capacity to lead in high-stakes environments. A model dialogue is also included for reference.

> **TEACHER NOTES:** *Expansion activities can be more effective when done with a partner, allowing you to practice the language and skills learned in this lesson more fully. If you don't have a teacher, consider practicing with a colleague or friend. Online teachers and tutors are also available at very reasonable rates these days. If you would like teacher notes to support your learning journey, just send an email to **prospeak.author@outlook.com**, and we'll be happy to send you a PDF containing additional task notes, example responses, and expansion activity guidelines.*

UNIT | **10 Effective Communication in Big Tech**

| Role A | Role: **Bill - Director L&D** |

Follow-up Meeting: Preparing for Stakeholder Questions

Background

As the Director of Learning and Development, you're tasked with ensuring that both the presentation content and team readiness meet the highest standards for the upcoming stakeholder meeting. Your primary goal is to develop content that effectively communicates strategic initiatives and prepares the team to handle stakeholder questions clearly and concisely.

Prompts

Propose conducting a mock Q&A session to practice responses to anticipated stakeholder questions, focusing particularly on strategic initiatives and long-term development plans.

Discuss strategies to project confidence and authority when presenting and responding to questions. Consider potential scenarios, such as unexpected queries regarding future projects.

Oversee the final preparations for the meeting, ensuring that all presentation materials are polished and that the team clearly understands their roles and responsibilities. Discuss backup plans for any unforeseen issues on the presentation day.

NOTES

UNIT | **10 Effective Communication in Big Tech**

NOTES

_____

. . . .

. . . .

. . . .

. . . .

. . . .

. . . .

. . . .

| **Role B** | Role: **Linda - Tech Team Manager** |

Follow-up Meeting: Preparing for Stakeholder Questions

Background

As the Tech Team Manager, your responsibility is to integrate the latest technical developments into the presentation effectively. You collaborate closely with Bill to ensure that the presentation not only covers all technical bases but also aligns with the Learning and Development department's goals for technical and business skills training.

Prompts

Prepare detailed updates about the latest technological advancements, such as enhancements in encryption and AI integration, to be included in the presentation. Ensure these updates are understandable to a non-technical audience.

Suggest ways to demonstrate the company's commitment to cutting-edge technology and relevant training to stay current with new technologies during the presentation. Suggest the inclusion of live demonstrations or recent project highlights.

Coordinate with Bill to set up a rehearsal schedule. Prepare to lead the technical portion of the presentation and discuss how to effectively address any complex questions from stakeholders.

ENGLISH AT THE SPEED OF TECH

ROLE-PLAY/SIMULATION - SAMPLE DIALOGUE

Bill: Hi Linda, I appreciate you meeting me on short notice. With the stakeholder meeting looming, we need to ensure our presentation not only informs but also impresses. How's the executive summary shaping up?

Linda: *Hi Bill, I've just finished integrating the latest on AI and encryption enhancements. The executive summary is concise and highlights our key achievements and strategic direction. It's ready for your review.*

Bill: That's great to hear. What if we conduct a mock Q&A session later this week? It could help us fine-tune our responses, especially for any unexpected questions about our future projects.

Linda: *Absolutely, a mock session would be invaluable. I'll prepare potential questions on our AI integration and its role in our sustainability commitments.*

Bill: Perfect. We also need to ensure that all presentation materials are polished and everyone is clear on their roles for the Q&A.

Linda: *Sure. Let's include the Q&A in our mock session. I'll double-check that the presentation is specific and aligned with our objectives. Also, I think a live demo could effectively highlight some of our recent technological advances.*

Bill: A live demo sounds brilliant, Linda. Could you handle that? It will definitely showcase our cutting-edge technology. Let's plan a rehearsal for Tuesday, so we can review everything and make any necessary adjustments.

Linda: *No problem. I'll coordinate with the tech team for the demo and prepare the final presentation for our rehearsal.*

Bill: Thank you, Linda. Your preparation has been outstanding!

Linda: *Thanks, Bill. I'll make sure everything is set for Tuesday.*

Expansion - Communication Strategy Plan

Develop a communication plan for improving internal communications. Use conditionals to outline potential scenarios and solutions, such as, "If we initiate weekly briefings, we can enhance team cohesion."

Objectives: Define your communication plan and how it aligns with business objectives.

Strategies: Specify the methods and outline potential advantages, such as faster project turnaround times or improved stakeholder satisfaction.

Challenges: Identify possible obstacles and how they can be mitigated.

Practice: Prepare and deliver your plan in a concise 3-minute presentation. Aim to clearly articulate your communication strategies using conditionals to explore hypothetical improvements. This can be done individually or with feedback from a partner or teacher for improvement. Good luck!

KEY VOCABULARY IN CONTEXT

Q1: If we include an executive summary, it will provide a snapshot of our *strategic* direction.

Incorrect: a) algorithm is a noun, but does not fit this context.

Incorrect: c) interface is a noun, but does not fit this context.

Q2: She effectively articulated the project scope to *stakeholders* yesterday.

Incorrect: a) encrypt is a verb, but does not fit this context.

Incorrect: b) monitored is a verb, but does not fit this context.

Q3: Our team has been ensuring stakeholders get complete *updates* this quarter.

Incorrect: b) clarify is a verb, not an adjective as needed here.

Incorrect: c) monetize is a verb, not an adjective.

Q4: If we set clear action items, everyone will know their *responsibilities*.

Incorrect: a) modularity is a noun, but does not fit this context.

Incorrect: b) encryption is a noun, but does not fit this context.

Q5: Our team has been defining specific goals to improve *focus*.

Incorrect: a) encrypted is a verb, not an adjective as is needed here.

Incorrect: c) monitored is a verb, not an adjective.

Q6: Taking regular meeting minutes has helped *clarify* decision-making processes.

Incorrect: b) prototype is a noun, but does not fit this context.

Incorrect: c) sponsorship is a noun, but does not fit this context.

Q7: If you summarize decisions and main ideas, we can ensure *consensus*.

Incorrect: a) traction is a noun, not a verb as is needed here.

Incorrect: b) prototype is a noun, not a verb.

Q8: We have been *focusing* on clear communication to prevent misunderstandings.

Incorrect: a) automate is a verb, not an adjective as is needed here.

Incorrect: b) iterate is a verb, not an adjective.

Q9: Being clear and concise in her presentation helped win *stakeholder* approval.

Incorrect: a) scalable is an adjective, but does not fit this context.

Incorrect: b) viral is an adjective, but does not fit this context.

Q10: If you can successfully convey the *benefits*, securing approval becomes easier.

Incorrect: a) interact is a verb, but does not fit this context.

Incorrect: b) debug is a verb, but does not fit this context.

NOTE: words in sentences 1-10 in *italics* are spaced repetition key words from previous units.

ENGLISH AT THE SPEED OF TECH

UNIT 10 Answer Key

BUSINESS DIALOGUE COMPREHENSION

Q1: What is the main purpose of the executive summary Linda plans to include?
• *Linda mentions that an executive summary will "set the right tone" and highlight the main achievements and plans of the company.*

Q2: Why is it important for each slide to have concise headings and bullet points according to Bill?
• *Bill emphasizes that concise headings and bullet points will help maintain clarity and engagement during the presentation.*

Q3: What additional content does Linda propose to include in the presentation if there is enough time?
• *Key encryption enhancements and interface updates for wearables - doing so will provide a more complete update on the company's technological advancements.*

Q4: What does Bill suggest to prepare for the Q&A session of the presentation?
• *Bill suggests assigning roles and be prepared for any questions on network security updates and AI integration.*

GRAMMAR PRACTICE

1. **(Except)** Unless we secure more funding, project expansion will be cancelled.
2. **(Prob)** If we automate these tasks, overall efficiency will increase.
3. **(Cert)** When you complete the course, your skills will be updated.
4. **(Prob)** If we invest in AI, our data analysis will be faster.
5. **(Except)** Unless we comply with regulations, penalties may be incurred.
6. **(Prob)** If we upgrade our servers, response times will improve.
7. **(Prob)** If we adopt blockchain, transaction security will be enhanced.
8. **(Cert)** When we finalize this deal, our market share will expand.
9. **(Except)** Unless we update our software, system vulnerabilities will remain.
10. **(Prob)** If we train employees now, future performance will benefit.

GRAMMAR IN ACTION: USING CONDITIONALS

Example model answers:
Contract Renewal: A vendor wants to increase service fees by 20%.
Example: *"If you keep the current fee, we can extend the contract for another two years."*
Yours: "If you agree to 10% instead of 20%, we can commit to a longer-term contract."
Yours: "If you provide some additional services, we can agree to the proposed increase."

Upgrade Request: Your manager is hesitant to approve an upgrade due to budget constraints.
Example: *"Unless we make the hardware upgrade, uptime can't be guaranteed."*
Yours: "If we allocate budget from other projects, can we cover the cost of the upgrade?"
Yours: "Unless we make this upgrade, we face system downtimes that will affect client services."

Revision Requirement: A contractor is required to make a revision before payment.
Example: *"When the revisions meet product specs, your invoice can be processed."*
Yours: *"When the changes have been verified, we will proceed with the payment."*
Yours: *"If you complete revisions by the end of the week, we can expedite payment."*

Unit 10 Notes

....
....
....
....
....
....
....
....

Key takeaways

....
....
....
....

Useful Vocabulary

Use the text boxes below to write the word or phrase on the left and how it was used on the right.

Key words	Example sentence

Useful phrases	Example sentence